Protecting Your Money
in the
Stock Market

It's a Herd Game!

Steve Godwin

Rev. date: 09/10/2015

To order additional copies of this book, contact:
Xlibris
1-888-795-4274
www.Xlibris.com
Orders@Xlibris.com
700735

Contents

APPRECIATION

To my friends Robert and Danny, who planted the seed to write. To my many students who asked questions that made me think. To my business partner, Jon, for always respectively listening to my ideas for the last 12 years. To my wife for her support and encouragement as I stumbled through the stock market Serengeti, cutting brush, fighting back lions, and sidestepping crocodiles for decades.

To Dr. Ed Yardeni, Marty Zweig, Norman Fosbach, and John Mauldin, educators who shared their knowledge in books and online freely. They made me a fortune.

LIST OF FIGURES

LIST OF TABLES

PREFACE

In order to survive, each new generation of investor must arm himself or herself with basic knowledge about the history, the numbers, and the people behind their investments. Each generation has to penetrate the misperceptions, mythology, and more importantly, the smoke and mirrors of Wall Street. These misperceptions have been perpetuated by too much emphasis on stock picking; too little emphasis on the big picture (history, numbers, and intermarket relationships); and virtually no attention to the psychological stress of investing over a lifetime.

INTRODUCTION

For 46 years, the stock market has been my window to the world. In the beginning (1968), it was a looking glass on the American form of capitalism. Near the end, it was a pan of global political and economic competition. In the beginning, I worked on learning what was economically important to the stock market. Now I use the stock market to explain what is economically important to me. Like the ocean, you can coexist in the markets, make money on it, and have fun on it and in it. However, like the ocean, you can never really conquer it. The stock market is constantly demanding new skills, new ideas, new approaches, and above all, humility. Hubris all but guarantees that sooner or later, you will have your head handed to you.

The purpose of this book is to share my adventure and to bring light on the best ideas and thinking I was exposed to during my journey. During my 46 years in the stock market, I have seen methodologies and people gain fame for having found the holy grail of stock market prediction, only to see them flame out a decade later. This book is really a collection of ideas from others that were functional in the beginning and are still viable today. The book is structured around a series of lectures I've given for the past 19 years at various community colleges in the San Francisco Bay Area. I'm an engineer by education and training. Consequently, my approach to the market is based on data, graphs, and light statistics. This is the language of the market. Try to embrace it; it will be worth your effort.

Like so many other baby boomers, I had various accounts with major brokerage firms over the decades. I was always searching for that wise, old stockbroker who was going to reveal the secrets of the markets.
I never found him at the brokerage firms and never made a dime there. By the time I left IBM in the mid-1990s, I knew more about the market

than 90% of the brokers I ever met. In 1995, I got my Series 7 license and became a part-time broker. I wanted to hit the ground running when I retired in 1996.

As a broker, I was appalled and stunned by what I ran into. I found that I had nothing in common with the brokers sitting beside me. I quickly learned that I was interested in making a million bucks beating the market. They were interested in making a million bucks selling the market. I spent my time trying to make my clients money; they spent their time trying to sell their clients something. Some brokerage firms have a team of experts located out of sight that advise the broker on what to buy or sell. I never could figure out how someone who didn't understand the market could interpret and tailor that advice to fit the customer's needs.

Consequently, I began telling myself that the customer needs to be warned. He needs to know what really goes on in the financial services industry. He needs to know that the game is legal but that it is set up to make the financial service industry money, not him. He needs to know the numbers are legal but only telling half the story. He needs to know the game is not about stock picking but about macroeconomic forces. He needs to know the big picture, including the type of people he is dealing with. To be sure, there are many good people in the industry who are knowledgeable, have integrity, and are looking out for the best interest of their clients. The lectures and this book are intended to help you find them.

Finally, there is good stuff here too. Once I've sensitized you to the dangers of the market, the later chapters show the tools, the logic, and the resources you will need to survive and maybe even prosper in the markets. The chapters are intended to be stand-alone but do have a flow. I'll end the introduction with the first and best advice ever given to me: **Start in the markets when you have very little money and make your mistakes as cheaply as possible.** I've made every mistake you are going to make and survived, even prospered with the ideas in this book.

Good luck on your adventure!

TRADERS CRY....

I WANT TO SEE THE PANIC. I WANT TO SMELL THE FEAR!

I WANT TO HEAR THE VEHEMENT REFUTATION OF THE CALL TO BUY.

I WANT A 'V' BOTTOM THAT SMACKS INTO SUPPORT LIKE A HAMMER ON AN ANVIL!

I WANT THE RISK RUNG OUT OF THE MARKET LIKE THE SWEAT WRUNG OUT OF THE LAST HANKY BY THE TREMBLING HANDS THAT JUST SOLD THEIR LAST STOCK

SO SURE WERE THEY THAT THE MARKET WAS GOING DOWN FROM HERE....

THEN I'LL BUY !

CHAPTER ONE

Myth Number 1: It's about Picking Great Companies

When you first come to the stock market, you may pick up a book, query your new stockbroker, or just comb through the newspapers, trying to understand the game. It's the rare exception that you don't end up believing that the game is about finding high-quality companies with good earnings, solid revenue stream, market dominance, etc. To add legitimacy, we in the industry add numbers (to the 2nd decimal) and ratios such as price/earnings (P/E), price/sales (P/S), price/book (P/B), etc., to guide you to those undiscovered gems. This is a trap. This gets you focusing in a narrow field of view, leaving you susceptible to periodic macroeconomic tsunamis. The real determinant of investment returns is asset allocation. Indeed, Beebower, Brinson, and Hood ("The Primary Determinant of Portfolio Return Variations," 1986[1]) reveal that asset allocation is 100% determinant of portfolio returns and 95% determinant of portfolio return variation (standard deviation). Wall Street continues to perpetuate the myth of stock selection as the entry to performance. Don't buy into it. We will delve into this subject more in later chapters.

Examples of the asset classes we have to work with today include the following:

• **Stocks**

Large company stocks
Small company stocks

Emerging market stocks
Developed country stocks

• Bonds and Cash Equivalents

Corporate bonds (high yield)
US government bonds, bills, notes
International developed country bonds
State and local government bonds
International emerging country bonds
Certificate of deposits

• Real Assets

Gold and silver
Commodities
Real estate

• Insurance Products

Fixed annuities
Guaranteed principal protected securities
Variable annuities

Now that I have your head up and focusing outward, you need to know that all asset classes are interrelated. Sometimes, these interrelationships are direct and intuitive such as those between interest rates (bond yields) and stock valuations, which we will talk about in later chapters. Other times, the relationships are ambiguous and complex, such as those between commodities and stock prices. Remember, each asset class is competing for your investment dollar. **Your task is to find the asset class that offers the best reward and lowest risk that's satisfactory to you, not Wall Street.** Wall Street knows this, and it's time for you to know it.

This book is about the stock market, so our primary focus is there. Comparing asset class performance (figure 1.1), we see that small capitalization (cap) stocks outperformed large capitalization stocks, government bonds and notes, and inflation over the last 87 years. Stocks have outperformed fixed income assets and inflation hands down. This data is the how and why money comes to the stock market. This is the data that helps stockbrokers sell you the market. We all want to obtain the best possible returns for our 401(k)s and our investment dollars. We all end up at the same watering hole.

Figure 1.1. Asset class performance[2]

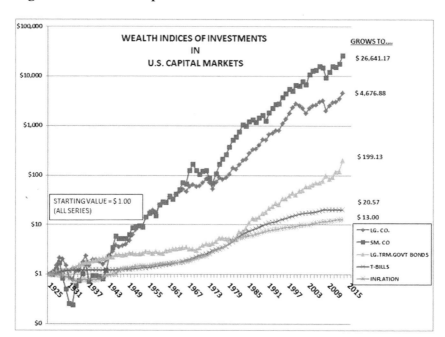

Data source: *Ibbotson SBBI 2014 Classic Yearbook*

What's interesting (we'll save for later discussion) is that the financial services industry knows this data yet continues to put most client money in large capitalization stocks. Indeed, Morningstar[3] shows for 2013 that there are 4,387 large-cap mutual funds diversified across 1,620 stocks, 1,497 midcap mutual funds diversified across 2019 stocks, and only 1,710 small-cap mutual funds across 5,868 stocks. When you realize that the large-cap funds account for about 75% of the total industry monies, you now know that the mutual fund industry is not as diversified as one might think.

There's a reason money is concentrated in large-cap funds. Several times a month, large sums (billions) of monies come in from retirement and pension plans. Mutual funds have to invest this money, and it's very difficult to insert the monies into small-cap stocks without impacting the stock price. A large-cap growth stock like Microsoft ($300 billion market cap) or Google ($196 billion market cap) can easily absorb a few billion dollars without impacting the stock price over the long term. So money flows into large-cap growth as means of convenience and not necessarily because of great stock value.

Definitions:

> **Size (small/large) = (outstanding shares × closing price) = market cap**
>
> **Growth/Value style**
>
> **A fundamental ratio, such as P/B and P/E, applied to a grouping of stocks**
>
> **Where price to book value (P/B) and price to earnings (P/E) are ratios used by analysts to measures whether a stock is overvalued or undervalued relative to some standard.**

The small-cap outperformance comes with a cost. That cost is increased volatility (risk).

No. Not a greater chance of loss but rather a greater variation of monthly returns around the mean return. I've given you the definition of risk in table 1.2.

More Definitions:

> For a series of asset returns, the standard deviation is a measure of risk.
>
> Standard deviation is calculated from the trailing twelve-month (monthly) price change. The standard deviation is a measure of the variation of price changes around an average or mean.
>
> All things being equal, lower standard deviation implies less risk.

An easy way to understand risk as defined here is to look at figure 1.2. The variations of monthly returns are shown for small, mid, and large caps from 2000 to 2006 (hypothetical). Note that in the main, all the caps move together, but that small and mid caps tend to move up more and down more than their large-cap brethren do. From 1926 to 2013, Morningstar reports[4] that the standard deviations are 19%, 28.8%, 8.4%, .9%, and 0% for large caps, small caps, government bonds, T-bills, and inflation, respectively.

Those great returns for small caps bring a 50% increase in volatility over large caps. So the next time you discuss risk with your broker, you now know he is talking volatility (standard deviation), not a chance of loss.

Figure 1.2. Volatility of returns (hypothetical returns)

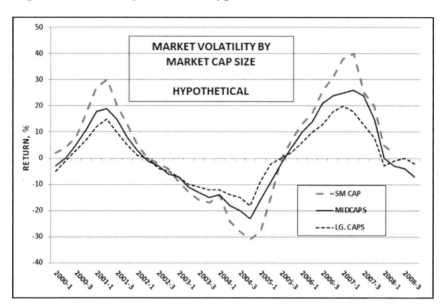

So what have we learned? Stocks can be subdivided into asset classes by size (market capitalization). Smaller cap stocks have outperformed large caps, bonds, bills, and inflation for over 80 years. Remember, a fundamental reason for investing is to protect the purchasing power (keep up with inflation) of our savings. You now know that performance brings risk (volatility). Your task is to balance performance with risk that is tolerable to you. You have to be able to sleep nights.

There is another subclass of stocks called growth and value (styles). Several firms, namely Standard & Poor's (S&P), Russell Investments, and others, have developed indexes based on these two fundamental partitions.

Figure 1.3 is an example of how Standard & Poor's created value and growth indices for the S&P 500 back in 2002. The S&P 500 index had a market cap of about $10.5 trillion. They created two buckets and filled the first bucket with the highest price to book ratio stocks (in the index) until they reached approximately half the $10.5 trillion. The residual stocks were placed in the second bucket. The first bucket is called growth, and the second bucket is called value. Note that growth doesn't mean earnings per share growth rates. Growth here is an accounting term. Also, notice the number of companies in the growth bucket (148) and value bucket (352). The growth bucket contains fewer companies than value, which means they are (typically) the larger market caps. We will discuss this more in a minute.

In some indices, you may see the same stock in both the value and growth components. In this case, the index vendor has used a proprietary calculation to weigh the stock more in one subindex than the other. They are saying that the stock has both growth and value attributes. Ugh! Man is ingenious at taking a simple idea and making it complex.

The partition of growth and value is arguably a partition by size. Many would argue that the two buckets are determined by fundamental values and size is incidental. I want you to be aware of size differential. Mid cap means a size of stocks near the middle of the total stock market capitalization range, and value denotes the smaller-cap stocks within that size range. Just to convince you that style ultimately means size, look at table 1.1.

Figure 1.3. Creating growth and value indices

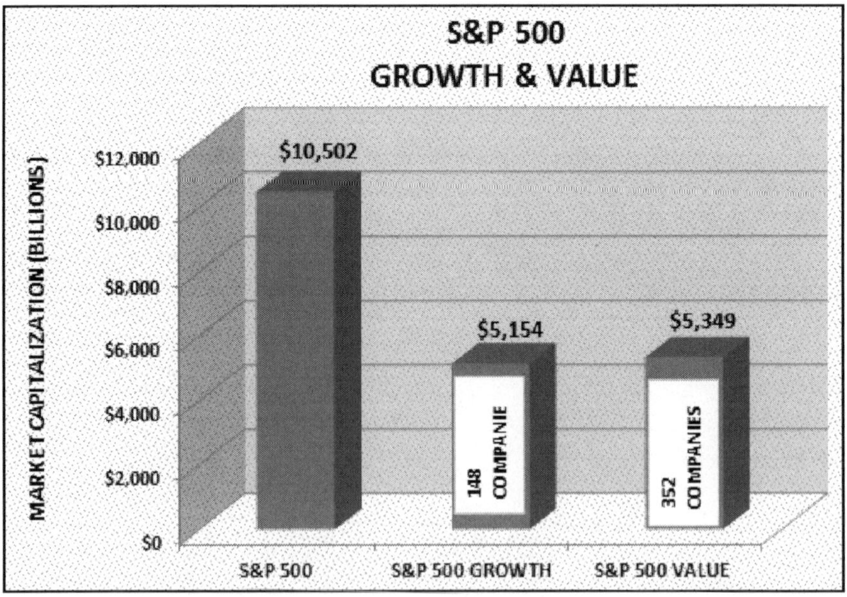

Data source: Standard & Poor's analysis as of March 31, 2002

The columns delineate the three market caps sizes and their styles

as defined by Standard & Poor's. The first row shows the number of stocks in each index. There are more stocks in each value component (meaning smaller market cap). The next two rows are the mean and median (midpoint) market caps of the indexes. Comparing, it's easy to see that value stocks have smaller market cap values in each index. Think size. It's a size game.

Table 1.1. Size of S&P styles (March 31, 2014)[5]

	S&P 500 Large-Cap Index		S&P 400 Midcap Index	S&P 600 Small-Cap Index
	Growth/ Value		Growth / Value	Growth/ Value
# of stocks	337	339	246 / 291	359 / 447
Mean Total Mkt. Cap ($millions)	35,247.9	34,566.0	4,499. / 3,818.	1,383. /1,169.
Median Total Mkt. Cap ($millions)	17,623.2	15,894.1	4,418. /3,454.	1,170. / 1,004.

Source: S&P Dow Jones Indices LLC

So what's the big deal? Let's buy small caps and move on with it. Figure 1.4 is the big deal. You now know that small caps outperformed (almost 6-fold) large caps over most of the 20th century. Figure 1.4 is illustrative of how the styles were performed. Here, we are using style series developed by French and Fama.[6] Note that small value (smallest of the small caps) had a whopping 53-fold outperformance over large growth (largest of the large caps) from 1927 to 2013. You probably won't be investing for 86 years, but you will be for a large chunk of that time.

Now you understand that the proper utilization of market cap size and style can have a huge impact on the ending value of your 401(k) at retirement.

Figure 1.4. Growth and value investing (1926–2013)[6]

Data source: *Ibbotson SBBI 2014 Classic Yearbook*

So what are typical small, mid, and large growth and value stocks? you ask. Let's take a look at Standard & Poor's size and style indices at the time of this writing. Table 1.2 is a snapshot of typical stocks from their lists.

Table 1.2. Typical size and style stocks[5]

Source: S&P Dow Jones Indices LLC

S&P 500 Large-Capitalization Growth / Value		S&P 400 Mid-Capitalization Growth / Value		S&P 600 Small-Capitalization Growth / Value	
Apple	Wells Fargo	Polaris	Ashland	FEI Company	Centene
Google	AT.T.	Under Armour	Foot Locker	Buffalo Wild	Emcor Group
Qualcomm	Exxon Mobil	Hanesbrands	Realty Income	Wings	
Comcast	Intel	United Rental	OGE Energy	Cognex Corp.	Treehouse Foods
Visa Inc.	Walmart				

This finishes our introduction to stock asset classes, but the nomenclature will be carried throughout the book. From this chapter, you now know that market capitalization size and style (defined as relative to size) are easy ways to think about and categorize market behavior and performance. You've learned that risk is not measured as a chance of loss; rather, it's a measure of volatility.

IS BETTER TO BE OUT OF

THE MARKET WANTING IN

THAN TO BE IN THE MARKET

WANTING OUT !

CHAPTER TWO

Myth Number 2: It's about Beating the Market

Most of us will be in a 401(k) or IRA (traditional or Roth) for years, if not decades. No doubt, you've seen brochures from mutual funds, financial advisors, or institutions advising you to invest for the long term. You've seen data or graphs alerting you to the fact that if you had missed the best month or day of returns over some investment period, you would have reduced portfolio returns significantly. These data are attempting to persuade you of the risk of attempting to time the market. This data is accurate and informative as far as it goes. Have you ever wondered that what may be more important to consider is what does missing the worst month or day of returns do to my overall portfolio returns?

The data in table 2.1 summarizes market data from 1926 to 2013. I used annual returns for large company stocks as reported in *Ibbotson SBBI 2014 Classic* Yearbook.[7] In this analysis, you have to understand that missing a few periods (best or worst) changes the order of returns. For example, the data shows that the average annual return for 1926–2013 for large companies was 11.8%. A dollar invested at the end of 1925 would have grown to $3999.36. The compound return was 9.8%. If we move the first 10 years to being the last ten years in the sequence, the average return stays the same, but our $1.00 now grows to $4673.63 for a compounded return of 10.1%. This is telling us that *sequence matters*. Now if we take the original sequence of years and pull out the best 5 single years, we get a huge reduction in returns. The average return drops to 9.6%, $1 grows to only

$654.10, and the compound return drops to 7.6%. So far, our data supports the conclusions in the glossy brochure your broker gave you (sort of).

Table 2.1. The effects of market timing[7]

	Average Return	$1 Grows to ...	Compound Return
1926-2013	11.8%	$3999.36	9.8%
Placing 1st 10 Years Last	11.8%	$4673.63	10.1%
Missing Best 5 Years	9.6%	$654.10	7.6%
Missing Worst 5 Years	14.6%	$ 36,493.86	12.8%
Missing Worst and Best 5 Years	12.6%	$5107.53	10.3%

Next, we look at what happens if we missed the worst 5 single years of returns. No, it's not an error. Your $1 does grow to $36,493.86, and your average and compounded returns go to 14.6 and 12.8%, respectively. All things being equal, the table is telling us two things. The first is that avoiding loss has a far greater impact to portfolio performance than missing the best returns. Second, sequence (order of returns) is huge, and it has a greater impact on compounded return than on average return.

Remember, the compounded return is the true measure of whether your wealth is increasing or decreasing. Also, realize that when you enter the workforce and when you retire can have huge effects on your ending wealth within the same demographics. So what's going on?

Let's look more at average annual return using table 2.2. Most financial industry data come at you in the form of average annual return. Items like total return or actual annual returns can be found but with difficulty. When you go onto the Internet looking for a small-cap fund, you will see screens with 1-, 3-, and 5-year performance with the heading "Average Annualized Returns." Look at table 2.2. I've given you sequences of 3 individual years of returns in each box. Each box nets out to an average return of 10%. Yet the geometric (compound) return varies from 10 to 6.3%.

Table 2.2. The magic of average annual returns

Year 1	+10%	Year 1	+ 5%	Year 1	+50%
Year 2	+10	Year 2	+10	Year 2	+0
Year 3	+10	Year 3	+15	Year 3	–20
Avg.	10%	Avg.	10%	Avg.	10%
Comp.	10%	Comp.	9.9%	Comp.	6.3%

One hundred dollars invested in each of the three sequences would have returned $133.10, $132.83, and $120 respectively. Compound returns are the measure of whether your wealth is increasing in value or not. Annualized returns are nice, easy to understand, ubiquitous, and useless for judging performance.

It's really important that you understand that *sequence has a huge impact on performance*. I've seen many a trading system (including mine) that looked good with back testing, optimization, and good money management that failed after performing Monte Carlo simulation (random sequencing). This short chapter should begin the sensitization process that things don't always appear as they seem. You need to look beyond and sometimes through the numbers presented to you by financial industry and the press.

Speaking of the press, let's close this chapter with an example of how the press can mislead you. The chart in figure 2.5 is from the St. Louis Federal Reserve website and was posted in 2008 in a leading business newspaper on the front page. The article inferred that the quantitative easing program enacted by the Federal Reserve during the financial crisis was really just a money-printing program. The article went on to explain that printing money would collapse the dollar, bring about rampant inflation, and economic chaos would follow. The solution, as reported in the article, was to own gold. This chart played into the panic emotions of the time and helped push gold prices to new highs. It helped sell newspapers too.

Figure 2.5. TWEXMMTH—US dollar index[8]

Source: FRED, Federal Reserve Bank of St. Louis

However, I enter into evidence another chart of the US dollar index (figure 2.6). This chart from FRED is of the same time period as before. What gives? Well this one is called the broad US dollar index. I'll explain the differences in just a minute.

Figure 2.6. TWEXBMTH—US dollar index (broad)[9]

Source: FRED, Federal Reserve Bank of St. Louis

If the negative correlation between gold and the dollar value was true, then we would have expected gold to have dropped in value during the long run-up of the dollar from the 1970s to the early 2000s. Look at figure 2.7 for the correlation or lack thereof. Indeed, gold went up with the rising dollar in the 1970s. It ran flat during the 1980s, '90s, and early 2000s, all periods of a rising dollar. In short, gold prices sometimes do correlate to a falling dollar, and other times, not. Indeed, I believe gold is a fear trade, not a dollar trade. But that's another story. Either way, predicting gold prices using the US dollar index would be a tough way to make a living.

Figure 2.7. London gold fixing in US dollars[10]

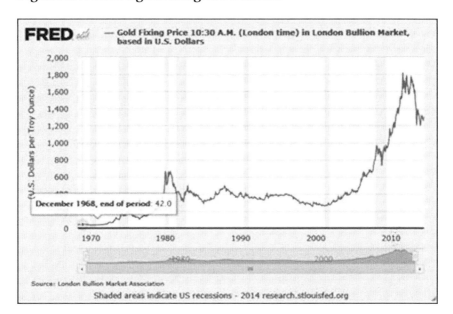

Source: FRED, Federal Reserve Bank of St. Louis

What the article left out was the description of the indexes, which I've included in tables 2.3 and 2.4 below. The first description is for figure 2.5, and the second is for figure 2.6. The first is narrowly defined for a few countries and the euro area. The second is for 25 countries and the euro area.

Which index do you think is more important? I think it depends on what you are trying to accomplish. If your focus is on developed economies, then probably you would use TWEXMMTH. If you're trying to understand how our currency is faring with developed plus emerging countries, then go with TWEXBMTH. Either way, you must understand how the graph was derived.

Table 2.3. TWEXMMTH—US dollar index[9]

Trade Weighted U.S. Dollar Index: Major Currencies

Averages of daily figures. A weighted average of the foreign exchange value of the U.S. dollar against a subset of the broad index currencies that circulate widely outside the country of issue. Major currency index includes the Euro Area, Canada, Japan, United Kingdom, Switzerland, Australia, and Sweden. For more information about trade-weighted indexes see http://www.federalreserve.gov/pubs/bulletin/2005/winter05_index.pdf.

Table 2.4. TWEXBMTH—US dollar index (broad)[10]

Averages of daily figures. A weighted average of the foreign exchange value of the U.S. dollar against the currencies of a broad group of major U.S. trading partners.
Broad currency index includes the Euro Area, Canada, Japan, Mexico, China, United Kingdom, Taiwan, Korea, Singapore, Hong Kong, Malaysia, Brazil, Switzerland, Thailand, Philippines, Australia, Indonesia, India, Israel, Saudi Arabia, Russia, Sweden, Argentina, Venezuela, Chile and Colombia.

My real point here is that the press and media can and will show you data and facts that play into the prevailing emotions of the street. Piling on to the fear and greed of the herd sells. You must question everything. *Telling half-truths is legal. You must ask, "What is not being said here?"*

SECRET OF THE MARKET :

MANY PEOPLE KNOW THE ANSWERS.

FIND PEOPLE WHO KNOW THE QUESTIONS !

CHAPTER THREE

Myth Number 3: It's about Earnings

So far, I've managed to keep your head up and looking at the broad picture. Let's drill down for a moment and focus on one of Wall Street's favorite subjects: *earnings*. As a preface to this discussion, let me point out that the stock market is a forward-looking animal. It's always looking at the tea leaves (data) and trying to discern the future of the economy, monetary policy, inflation, earnings, etc. Consequently, it is future earnings that are important, not the past. Really? Let's look at figure 3.1. It's a little complicated but provides a great perspective. Back in the heady days of the 1995–2000 bull market, analysts were predicting peak 12-month forward earnings (for year 2000) for the S&P 500 of about $63/share (left black circled area).

We all know what happened in 2000. The stock market tanked (Internet bubble burst), and earnings forecasts declined. Earnings estimates began rising after 2001. The bull market reignited in March of 2003. Note that in 2004, earnings forecast regained and even exceeded 2000 levels (right black circle). If the stock market is primarily driven by earnings, then we would have expected the market to have regained its 2000 peak around 2004. Let's see what happened.

Figure 3.1. Forward earnings[11]

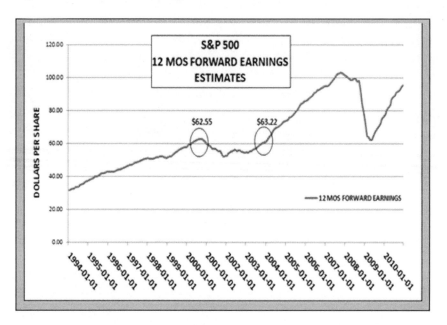

Data source: S&P Dow Jones Indices LLC

I enter into evidence a price chart of the S&P 500 in figure 3.2 with the S&P 500 for 2004 circled. Indeed, the S&P 500 didn't reach its 2000 level until late 2007. To add salt to the wound, look at the price performance of the Dow Jones Industrial Average (America's premier companies) during the same period (figure 3.3).

Figure 3.2. S&P 500 price performance 1995–2014

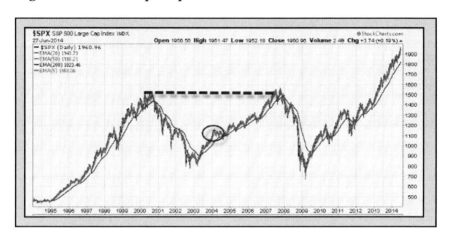

Source: StockCharts.com

The Dow didn't hit its previous high until 2007. Waiting 3–4 years for stocks to reflect previous forecast can be quite painful. Most investors don't have the patience or the capital to wait that long.

Every day, you hear people on financial talk shows telling the audience that their success has been due to buying quality companies with positive earnings trends. You see stock prices move, sometimes violently, after quarterly earnings are posted.

Figure 3.3, Dow Jones Industrial Average price performance 1995–2014

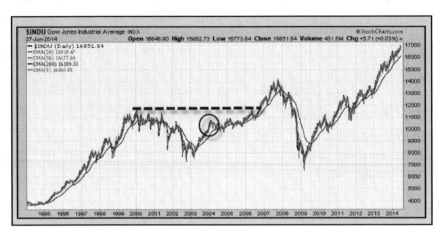

Source: StockCharts.Com

Surely, earnings are important? you ask. Let's take a look at the firms that use earnings and fundamental forecasting as primary tools for predicting stock direction and level. Let's look at 2 of the most successful Wall Street firms in US history. Let's look at Merrill Lynch and J. P. Morgan. Let's see how they did in the biggest bull market in US history (1995–2000) using Intel stock.

Figures 3.4 and 3.5 below are charts of Intel stock price from 1998 to 2014. I have buy and sell recommendations from J. P. Morgan and Merrill Lynch identified (arrows). The data was used with permission from Briefing.com and the Analyst Ratings Network websites on December 11, 2014. I chose J. P. Morgan and Merrill Lynch as they are still in business. From a list of 25 firms (table 3.1) analyzing Intel in 1998, I found only J. P. Morgan was making recommendations on Intel up to 2014.

Figure 3.4. Intel stock recommendations by J. P. Morgan[12]

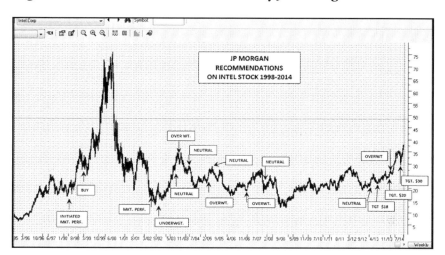

Data source: Analyst Ratings Network (with permission)

J. P. Morgan initiated coverage in April 1998 with a market perform on Intel stock. They put out a buy in January of 1999, just in time for the blow-off stage and demise of the bull in 2000. They kept you in through the collapse and subsequent decade. Their last recommendation, January 17, 2014, was for a target price of $30. As best I could tell, J. P. Morgan got you in 1999 at $25.68 per share. They kept you in for 15 years, and today, the price is $36.70. That's $11.02 (43%) profit in 15 years.

Figure 3.5. Intel stock recommendations by Merrill Lynch[12]

Data source: Analyst Ratings Network (with permission)

Figure 3.5 is the story of Merrill Lynch and its recommendations for Intel. This story begins in 1998 with a long-term accumulate recommendation. Like J. P. Morgan, Merrill gets you in and keeps you in for the 1998–1999 run-up but never gets you out. Merrill even got you to buy more (January 2002 was a strong buy) during the long run to the bottom in 2003. They gave you a sell at the bottom in November 2002 but came right back 6 months later with a buy in July of 2003.

Neither firm gives suitable guidance after the 2000 crash. I don't know about you, but terms like *neutral* or *underweight* just confuse me. Another thing to be gained from both charts is that the recommendations came like rapid-fire. Do you really think Intel's earnings outlooks were changing that rapidly? My point? Using earnings forecasting to predict stock prices didn't seem to help 2 of the biggest and most successful firms on the street make me money on Intel in the 1990s and beyond. I guess I was just supposed to be a long-term investor.

This brings up another issue I have with Wall Street. Many firms and many newsletters will get you into a stock and then walk away, leaving you holding the bag. I only subscribe to newsletters that display both buy and sell recommendations, not just buys.

Below is a list of the 25 firms using fundamentals (earnings) to predict the direction of Intel stock in 1998. Only a handful are left. So much for fundamental analysis and the wire houses and institutions that touted them.

Table 3.1. Companies with recommendations on Intel stock (1998–1999)[12]

Data source: Analyst Ratings Network (with permission)

BT Alex Brown	Volpe Brown
CIBC Oppenheimer	Sunlogic Securities
JP Morgan	Lehman Bros.
Morgan Stanley	Prudential
Merrill Lynch	AG Edwards
Sound View	Everen Securities
BA Robertson Stephens	Paine Webber
NB Montgomery	Dean Witter
Cowen & Co	Goldman Sachs
Piper Jaffray	Bank of America Secs
Bear Stearns	ABN AMRO
Salomon Smith Barney	CS First Boston
Gruntal & Co.	

Earnings have to count for something, you say. Yes, they do. Let's look at where this idea that earnings count comes from. Figure 3.6 gives us a long-term (1926–2014) view of price change (top graph) and earnings (second graph). Notice the correlation (two dotted lines) between price and earnings. Yes, stock prices do follow virtually the same trend as earnings but over decade if not century-long periods.

Focus again on figure 3.6. The slope of the earnings trend line has not changed much in 80 years. Then why did we have market crashes in 1974, 1987, 1997, 1998, 2000, and 2008? Why did we have the great bull markets of 1982, 1995, 2003, and 2009? Were they really earnings-driven? The answer lies in the third graph. *Stock prices are driven by what investors are willing to pay for a dollar of earnings.*

Figure 3.6. S&P 500 price, earnings, trailing P/E, and dividend yield (1926–2014)

Source: StockCharts.com

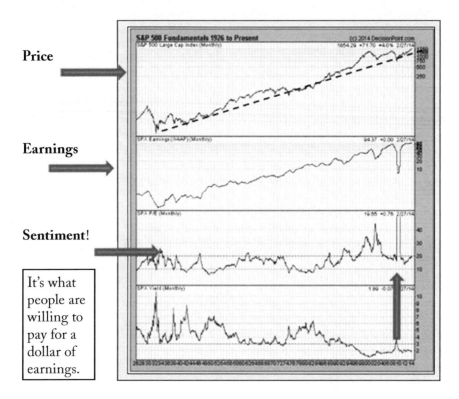

Price

Earnings

Sentiment!

It's what people are willing to pay for a dollar of earnings.

P/E, in this case, is another way of describing investor sentiment. A dollar of earnings is sometimes worth more to investors than other times. The beauty of earnings is in the eyes of the beholder.

Note that from 1926 to about 1995, the P/E ratio moved in a channel with approximately 20 as the upper bound and 10 as the lower bound. The channel is not exact but gives you a feel for what a dollar of earnings was worth over most of the 20th century. Look at the long upward trend in P/Es from the 1982 bottom to the peak in 2000. In 2000 (up arrow), investors felt that a dollar of earnings from the likes of Intel, Cisco, Microsoft, etc., was worth more than any dollar earnings in the 20th century. After the crash, in 2001, Intel Inc. reported earnings of $0.19 per share. The stock price hit bottom in September 2002 at a split adjusted $10.35. For the latest fiscal year (2013), Intel Inc. reported earnings per share of $1.89. At this writing (December 11, 2014), the stock closed at $36.70. That's a tenfold increase in earnings and a little more than a threefold increase in price over 12 years. Yet Intel Inc. continues to be a great company and a leader in its field. My comment is that if you want to enjoy Intel's earnings, then go to work for Intel. Don't buy the stock.

A lot of investors still don't know what happened. They believed that Intel, Cisco, and the other large-cap-growth companies of that era were great companies with products that were going to change the world. It was and is still true that these are great companies that will change the world. But investors paid too much for them, just as they paid too much for Polaroid, Kodak, Xerox, and the IBMs before them. Of the stock asset classes, you now know that large-cap growth was the worst performing.

Care to guess the P/E of some of today's darling large-cap growth stocks? I'm not the only analyst to ponder about the relationship between earnings and stock prices. Norman Fosback wrote a newsletter in the 1980s–1990s called *Market Logic*. In his February 1990 issue, he discussed his multifactor forecasting model for the stock market. His work focused on sentiment, fundamentals, technicals, and monetary policy. Sentiment has already been described as the price investors are willing to pay for a dollar of earnings but can be expanded to include the number of bullish versus bearish newsletters, surveys of investors' attitudes, consumer spending plans, and so on. Monetary policy is primarily about whether the central bank (the Fed) is stimulating or trying to slow the growth of the US economy. Fundamentals focus on corporate earnings and valuations. Technicals refer to mathematical indicators that capture stock price behavior relative to extremes. We will devote a whole chapter to technical indicators. But for now, go with the definition I've given. I've summarized his findings in figure 3.7.

Figure 3.7. What explains future stock price behavior?

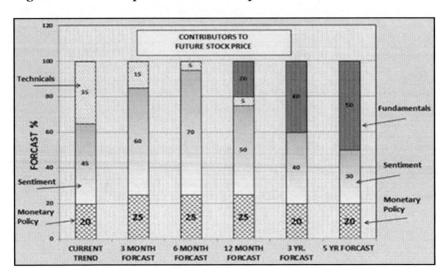

Fosback's work leads us to the stunning conclusion that when forecasting future stock prices, the primary short-term (< 6 months) determinants are sentiment, technicals, and monetary policy. Fundamentals don't enter into the forecast until about a year out. It's only at 3 years out that fundamentals have a significant role in forecasting stock price and then only at 40% weight. It's a rare investor who can wait 3 to 5 years for a stock to reflect an earnings projection by your local analyst.

In conclusion, earnings do count. They count in the seconds after an earnings announcement or a dividend increase announcement. They count for a few minutes after a CEO announces he will step down unexpectedly to spend more time with his family. They count if you're investing with a multiyear outlook. They really count if you're Rip Van Winkle sleeping with a 60- to-80-year outlook. But in between, *stock prices are driven by sentiment, monetary policy, and technicals.*

COMPANIES ARE DRIVEN BY EARNINGS.

STOCKS ARE DRIVEN BY SENTIMENT

OR

BY WHAT PEOPLE ARE WILLING TO PAY

FOR A DOLLARS' WORTH OF EARNINGS!

CHAPTER FOUR

If It's Not Stock Picking, What Is It?

Seeing the Big Picture

Up to this chapter, we have talked about stocks, asset classes, and performance. It's been about stocks all the way. In this chapter, I want to start the expansion of your thoughts to the other forces and relationships that drive stock price. To get going with the big picture, let's first look at typical market logic (figure 4.1). The economy expands ↑ or contracts ↓ , followed by an increase ↑ or decrease ↓ in corporate earnings. Stock prices soon follow in the direction of the economy and earnings. This is what most people believe, including most MBAs. This is all quite logical but wrong. What really happens is flow-charted in the second panel. Stock prices move in anticipation of the Federal Reserve's (FED) policy actions and how the economy is expected to react to that policy. This is why we call the market a forward discounting mechanism. *If you wait to see corporate earnings rise or fall before investing, you will be 12 to 18 months late.*

Figure 4.1. Market logic

Economy ↑↓ → Corporate earnings ↑↓ → Stock prices ↑↓

Logical but wrong!

What really happens is . . .

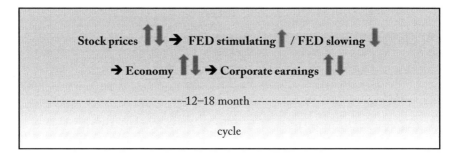

So the game is about watching and anticipating the Fed. It's about watching what the Fed is watching. The Federal Reserve has what is called a dual mandate. They are chartered to maintain stable prices (fight inflation) and to maximize employment in the domestic economy. They strive to achieve their goals with a variety of tools, primarily the increase or decrease of the US money supply and treasury interest rates. Historically, the Fed has manipulated short-term interest rates (i.e., T-bills, the discount rate, along with measures of money supply known as M1 and M2). However, since the 2008 financial crisis, the Fed has added new weapons to its arsenal by purchasing long-term mortgage debt obligations, government sponsored agencies, and treasury bonds. They have facilitated loans to investment banks and insurance companies and have pushed short-term interest rates to near zero. All this manipulation is rolled up into what is called *monetary policy.*

Before we dig into Fed behavior, I have set aside what I want you to tuck into your head. The United States government debt (treasury debt) is the safest debt on our planet. The treasury has never defaulted and is backed by the taxing authority of the richest nation in history. If you are any other entity on this planet and wanted to borrow money (float debt), you would have to pay interest to the debt holder at least at the US government rate plus some risk premium. When the Fed raises or lowers interest rates, all rates around the planet have to adjust. Think about this. There may be times (months, years) when comparative rates get out of correlation, but eventually, they will fall back to this fundamental relationship.

So what does the Fed watch? Of course, the Fed watches anything related to their mandate. You can study inflation parameters at the Bureau of Labor Statistics website.[13] An example of the types of data available is shown in figure 4.2. The data can be customized, graphed and best of all, is free.

Notice the two charts on the right side of figure 4.2. The upper chart is showing annual change in consumer prices (CPI) as measured for all items. The lower chart shows the CPI for all items less food and energy. The latter is usually the CPI you hear and read about in the local newspaper. What's the difference? *The Fed makes monetary policy decisions based on trends.* Pulling out food and energy costs tends to smooth the curve and reveal the underlying trend. That's all. They are not trying to hide anything as many would have you believe.

Figure 4.2. Types of inflation statistics

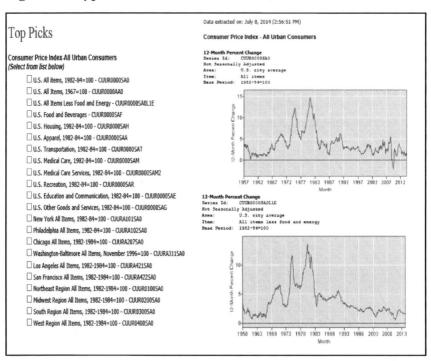

Source: Bureau of Labor Statistics[13]

The CPI represents changes in prices of all goods and service purchased by urban households. Sales and excise taxes are included. Income taxes are not included. The Bureau of Labor Statistics reports that the category of All Urban Consumers (CPI-U) covers about 87% of the US population. The category of Urban Wage Earners and Clerical Workers

(CPI-W) covers about 32% of the population. Indexes are available for groups of expenditures like food, beverages, medical care, education, and transportation. If you hear news on inflation and/or the stock market is moving on an inflation report, you can visit the website for the complete report. Sometimes, the press or the media gets it wrong. Take the time to visit this site. Don't memorize it, but learn what data is available if you need it. In particular, read the description of methodologies.

The Fed also watches us, the consumers, investors, and businesspeople. Expectations of inflation drive our decisions to consume (buy cars, homes, mortgages) now or later. Certainly, we wouldn't lend money to a corporation (buy corporate debt) to expand its manufacturing facility at 2% if we thought inflation would be 4% over the payback period. Inversely, a corporation wouldn't plan on investing in new equipment if the cost of the loan was going to be greater than the payback from the expansion. *Expectations on inflation drive our economy.* Thus, part of the Fed's work in managing inflation is to know and understand public perception of future inflation. Indeed, *an arcane function of the Fed is to manage confidence.* Confidence is a lubricant of any economy. People don't loan money unless they are confident they will be paid back. Businesses don't expand and hire new workers unless they have confidence it will pay off in the future. People don't marry, build families, and plan careers and college unless they feel confident that the future is economically stable and safe. You can monitor domestic *inflation expectations* by visiting the Federal Reserve Bank of Cleveland website.

As of June 17, 2014, the public expected inflation to average out at less than 2% over the next 10 years. The next time you hear a pundit on TV exclaim that everyone knows rampant inflation is just ahead or that the current Fed policy will inevitably lead to deflation, you can access this data to establish his credibility. This data will help keep you informed and calm, and it's all part of Fed watch. If investors, consumers, and businesspeople are confident that inflation is not a future problem, then the Fed feels good about their inflation-directed policy. This means that they are not likely to make big monetary moves anytime soon. If the Fed feels good, you should feel good.

As stated, confidence in economic policy is crucial to the success of any Fed. There is even an economic policy uncertainty index in the FRED database and shown in figure 4.3. This is based on work by Baker, Bloom, and Davis[14] and adds emphasis to my point that the economy is not just

---

about managing numbers but also contains abstract qualities that have to be dealt with.

Note the spikes in uncertainty around the 9/11 event in 2001 and again in the 2008 financial meltdown. To close the subject of inflation fighting, let me make you aware that there are many indicators besides the CPI. Indicators such as the personal consumption expenditure (PCE) index (a favorite of the Fed) and GDP price deflator can be monitored. The CPI is basically a fixed basket of goods, whereas the PCE attempts to contain a variable basket that reflects changing consumer buying pattern.

Figure 4.3. Economic policy uncertainty index for the United States[14]

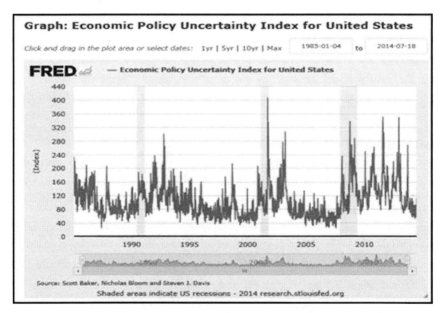

Source: FRED, Federal Reserve Bank of St. Louis

The GDP price deflator is a very broad measure of how much the change in domestic GDP can be attributed to price appreciation versus actual increase due to output.

Now let's turn to the second Fed mandate of maximizing employment. Employment data can be found at the same website as where the inflation data can be found and is shown in figure 4.4. The press and the media will typically report on unemployment, so let's focus there. Over the years, I've heard many times that the government is not measuring the true unemployment rate, that they are hiding something. Don't listen to that stuff; don't generalize. Go find out for yourself. There are 35 different data sets in figure 4.4. The 2 graphs show the unemployment rate for all males over 20 years (top graph) and that for college grads over 25 years of age (bottom graph). As of June 26, 2014, those numbers would be about 6.1% and 3.2% respectively. Education still appears to offer an advantage in employment. So now you know where the data is located. There is no excuse for being misled or surprised by inflation and/or unemployment figures reported in the press and media

Perhaps *the most important tool you have for watching the Fed is interest rates*. Interest rates tend to be the focal point of Fed action. They can alter monetary policy by means of other tools (i.e., money supply), but interest rates ultimately tell the tale. Long-term interest rates can also give you a sense of the direction of the economy. Finally, the interest rate (fixed income) market is also a collection of investors. Monitoring the fixed income market gives insight as to their view of the economy and impending Fed action.

Figure 4.4. Employment statistics—Bureau of Labor Statistics[15]

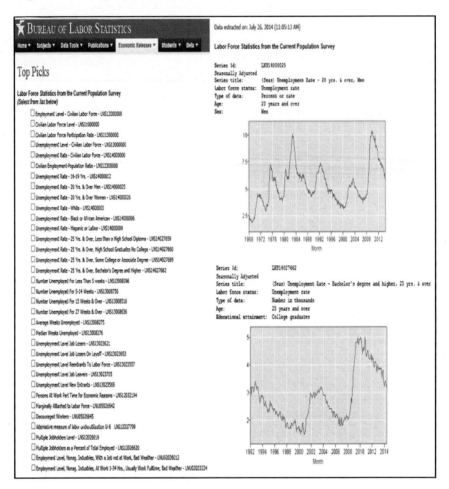

Source: Bureau of Labor Statistics

Figure 4.5 shows the yield (interest rate) on 10-year treasury bonds and the annualized change in nominal GDP[16] (nominal meaning not corrected for inflation by the GDP deflator). Notice how the two track over the long term but zig and zag around each other in the short term. Also, notice that prior to the 1980s, investors were willing to accept 10-year rates less than the GDP rate of change. After the 1980s, they demanded 10-year rates above GDP rate of change. This is because the country experienced high inflation in the 1970s and investors wanted higher yield to compensate for perceived inflation risk going forward into the 1980s. Since the 1980s, the

Fed has been able to suppress inflation, and rates are now down about equal to GDP rate of change.

This brings up an important point. It is not sufficient to collect data into a spreadsheet and run statistics without understanding the context of the economic environment. Over decades, many statistics average out to tell you nothing. *Understanding the context of the current economic environment will help you select past data most comparable.* This isn't cheating. A lot of past data is outlier because of context. However, sometimes, what appears to be outlier data can be used to discern where the markets are going. I'll explain next.

Figure 4.5. Interest rates and the economy (1947–2014)[16]

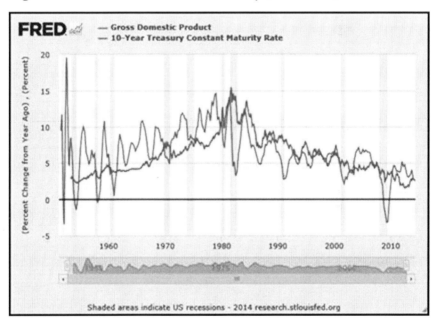

Chart source: FRED, Federal Reserve Bank of St. Louis

One of my favorite tools is a simple model that compares interest rates (10-year treasury bonds) and corporate earnings to existing stock (S&P 500) prices. It's a piece of Fed watch and helps with context. Figure 4.6 is a time series graph of the 10-year treasury bond (downsloping line) yields alongside the forward earnings yield (down then up line) for the S&P 500.

More definitions:

Earnings yield = 1 / PE Ratio = E / P

where E = 12 months forward earnings estimates

and P = today's closing price for the S&P 500 index

Figure 4.6. Forward earnings yield and 10-year treasury bond rates (1979–2014)[17]

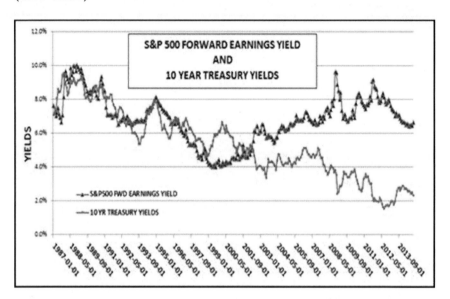

Data source: FRED, St. Louis Federal Reserve, Yardeni Research Inc.

Prior to the early 2000s, the two lines tracked each other and gave rise to a stock valuation model. Dr. Ed Yardeni takes credit for digging the model out of a Humphrey-Hawkins report to Congress in 1997[18] and dubbing it the *Fed model*. Simply put, *the model expresses the fair value price of the S&P 500 given the forward estimated outlook for earnings and the current yield on 10-year treasury bonds.* Here is what it looks like in formula form:

$$P_{(fv)} = E_f / Y$$

Where $P_{(fv)}$ = S&P 500 fair value price

E_f = estimated forward earnings

Y = yield on 10-year treasury bond

If current P < P$_{(fv)}$, stocks are undervalued

If current P > P$_{(fv)}$, stocks are overvalued

At the time of this writing, the forward estimates for the S&P 500 are $137.49 and the yield on the 10-year treasury is 2.58%. The model gives a fair value estimate of $5,329 per share. The current price is $1,978 or 63% undervalued. I've plotted this over-under valuation model back to 1987 (figure 4.7). I've put a star on the chart to show the current position as of July 2014.

Figure 4.7. Fed valuation model (1979–2014)[17]

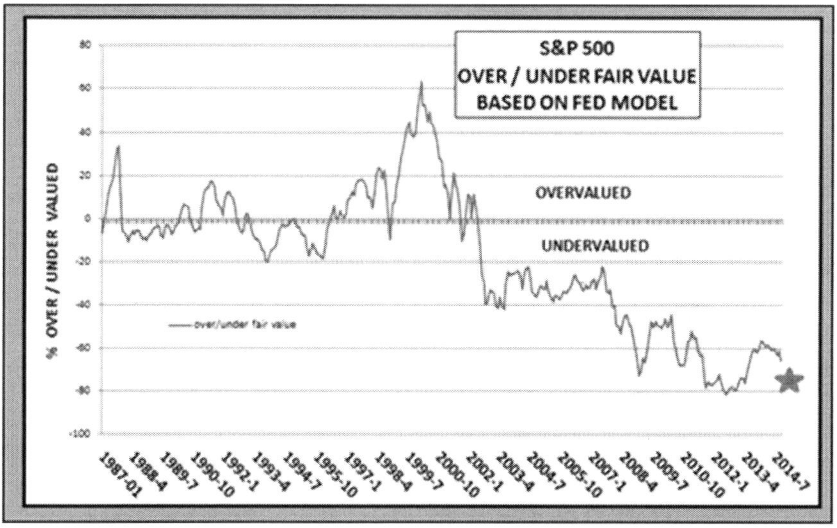

After Dr. Ed Yardeni

Stocks are dirt cheap, you say. But yes, the reason this model is telling us that stocks are cheap is that the Fed has lowered the yield on the 10-year treasury bond to get us through the financial crisis of 2008. Some would say that because the data is artificially driven by temporary Fed policy, it should be considered outlier and not useful. Not so. The utility of the model is that it allows you to dial in what-if changes in interest rates and earnings to see where you are and where you can be hurt. Interest rates can and will rise, but earnings can rise too. How far can rates rise before you get into overvalued territory? How much do earnings have to improve to balance rising rates? The model helps you answer these important questions.

Stocks and bonds are competing asset classes for the investor's discretionary income. When the earnings yield is above the bond yield, stocks are perceived by many as the better investment and vice versa. The model is not a timing model. Stocks have been undervalued going on 12 years at this writing. However, I don't know about you, but I'd much rather be dollar averaging into stocks in my 401(k) when stocks are this cheap than, say, in 1996–2000. Here's the point. You will hear pundits calling for a correction in stock prices because stocks are overvalued. Figure 4.7 is telling you that *stocks can go for years in overvalued and undervalued* regimes. You need to know where you are in valuation space if you are going to cope with the temptations and stress thrown at you by the media and press.

Let's go back to figure 4.6. Bond and earnings yield track fairly well up to about 2002 then diverge significantly. Many people have declared that the model is dead and no longer useful. Many investigators have created variations on the model, and the one with a great deal of merit is the capital structure substitution theory presented by Trimmer[19]. Essentially, this model is a restatement of the Fed model and predicts that corporations will be induced to buy back their stock when the earnings yield is greater than the cost to borrow minus the corporate tax rate.

$$E/P = R / (1-T)$$

Where E = earnings per share
R = yield on Moody's Aaa Bond Index
P = price per share
T = corporate tax rate

(3a) If current E/P > R / (1–T),   buy stock back

(3b) If current E/P < R / (1–T),   issue debt

Condition (3a) has been in effect since about 2002. Indeed, figure 4.8 is a chart showing the level of stock buybacks (bar chart) versus the spread between forward earnings yield and corporate Aaa bond yields (bottom chart). Based on the substitution model, we would expect the buybacks to continue.

Remember, reducing the float (increasing buybacks) is reducing supply. All things being equal, a reduction in supply with the same demand is very bullish for stocks. Indeed, TrimTabs Asset Management reports that there have been 9 periods of float shrink and expansion since 1984.[20] The average returns on the S&P 500 for the float shrink and expansion periods were 12.1% and –2.7% respectively. That's huge.

Figure 4.8. Stock buybacks and earnings yield—corporate bond yield (1987–2014)[21]

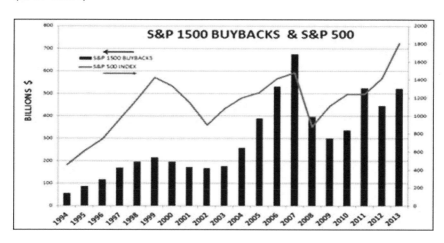

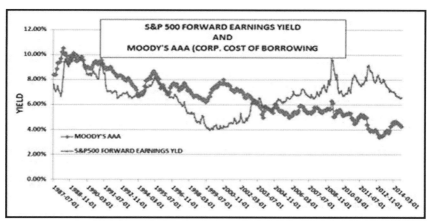

Source: S&P Dow Jones Indices
Data source: Yardeni Research Inc., FRED, St. Louis Federal Reserve Bank

Thus, the Fed model and its variations are handy tools by which to relate interest rates and earnings back to historical stock valuations and investment competitiveness. They also give insight as to the potential course of stock buybacks and mergers (supply). And it is a key piece of Fed watch. Tuck it into your back pocket, and take it with you.

As stated at the beginning of the chapter, another primary tool of Fed monetary policy is the manipulation of the money supply. This is an arcane process full of acronyms like interest rates on excess reserves (IOER) and reverse repurchase facility (RRF) or the term deposit facility (TDF). How these programs work and their intended goals are beyond the scope of this book and this author. However, we won't let it stop us from inspecting this aspect of Fed policy.

Primarily, the Fed injects money into the financial system by buying assets. Assets could be bonds, commercial paper, debt obligations, etc. By paying cash to institutions for these assets, they are essentially putting cash into the system. Buying treasury bonds from banks puts cash on the bank's balance sheet and is therefore available to be loaned. Banks actually create money when they loan. Banks are required to maintain a certain amount of money in reserve, and they can and do park this reserve cash back in the Fed's vault. If they maintain more reserves than is required by the fed, they are said to have excess reserves. The assets purchased by the Fed go to the Fed's balance sheet and are a proxy for stimulus in the economy. Deposited excess reserves go to the Fed balance sheet as a liability and are referred to as the monetary base or high-powered money.

What do we do with all this information? Well, we can observe the Fed's intentions by watching its balance sheet. If the asset side is growing, we know the Fed is injecting money into the financial system and vice versa. If the liability side (excess reserves) is growing, we know that banks aren't lending all that they can. Figures 4.9 is a nice summary chart of the Fed's assets and bank excess reserves.

Figure 4.9. Federal Reserve balance sheet and excess reserves[22]

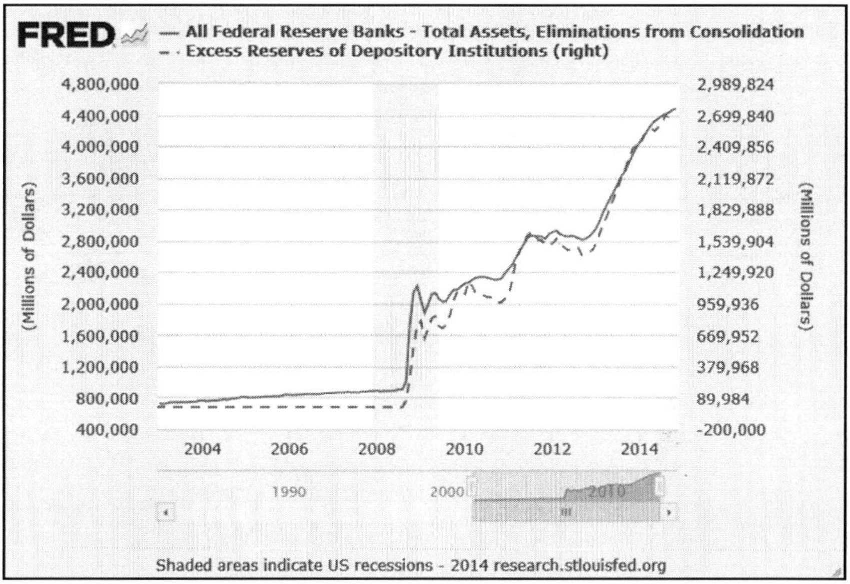

Source: FRED, Federal Reserve Bank of St. Louis

As we said early in the chapter, *stock prices ultimately reflect what people think the Fed is doing and what the outcome of that action will be to the economy and corporate earnings.* The press and media are constantly telling us what the Fed is thinking and doing and about to do. You must develop a way to monitor Fed actions. That's the only real way to determine Fed intentions and policy. Let me cement that idea into your brain with figure 4.10. What the Fed does is a market matter.

Figure 4.10. Fed balance sheet and the S&P 500 as of November 25, 2014[23]

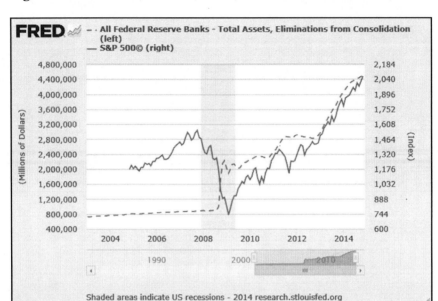

Source: FRED, Federal Reserve Bank of St. Louis

You should come out of this chapter with the knowledge that *the Fed is the key player* on your stock market team. You know that the Fed uses interest rates and money supply as key tools to drive the economy (monetary policy). You now know that interest rates have a direct bearing on stock market valuations and investment competitiveness. We began the process of broadening your view in this chapter. We will continue the process in later chapters.

CHAPTER FIVE

Modern Portfolio Theory or the Theory of Relativity

No, Einstein Wasn't Here

For those of you who grew up in science and engineering, you have 200 years of tested theory, dating back to Sir Isaac Newton. Modern portfolio theory has less than half that quantum of tested theory. Indeed, Markowitz is credited for driving the first stake in the ground in his 1952 paper entitled "Portfolio Selection." He was followed by Sharpe, Lintner, and Mossin in what developed as the *capital asset pricing model*. Later in the 1970s, the now-popular option valuation model of Black and Scholes was published. Perhaps the most arguable thrust in theory was by Fama with his *efficient market theory* in 1965. We can't forget Burton Malkiel with *Random Walk* (2003, 8th edition).

Briefly, my interpretation of the above work is genius. However, a lot of their ideas aren't directly applicable to the small portfolios you and I are working with. You would need their work if you were constructing highly theoretical portfolios for large institutions. In addition, some of their ideas don't hold up in practice. The efficient market theory proposes that information is disseminated into and everywhere in the market efficiently. It proposes that investors will rationally do that which is in their own best interest. It doesn't take long to shoot those concepts down. When information comes to the market, many investors misinterpret, some don't believe, and others reject the information no matter how factual. Looking at rationality, more people buy stocks when they are expensive than when they are cheap.

Just look at daily trading volumes at market tops versus bottoms. Indeed, most investors are loaded with *confirmation bias*, a cognitive perception bias that constricts the investor to focus on those facts and figures that confirm their preconceived beliefs. In this regard, I believe an ancillary task of the press and media is to discern the prevailing investor bias and then feed it with article after article. Many investigators have shown that particularly negative business magazine covers occur near market bottoms and vice versa.

If you get interested in investor psychology, search for *behavioral economics* on your Internet search engine. It's a relatively new branch of economics and a direct assault on many of the concepts proposed by Nobel laureates of the past. Not many good books have been written, but they are coming.

So what does theory hold for us? My net of it all is that you want to diversify, diversify, and diversify. Hold various asset classes that are all going up (hopefully) over time but are out of phase. Hopefully, some are trending up while others may be trendless or even dropping in value. This has the benefit of reducing overall portfolio volatility, but it may actually increase portfolio total returns over the longer time frame. An example of this behavior is shown in figure 5.1.

Figure 5.1. Asset classes with out-of-phase behavior

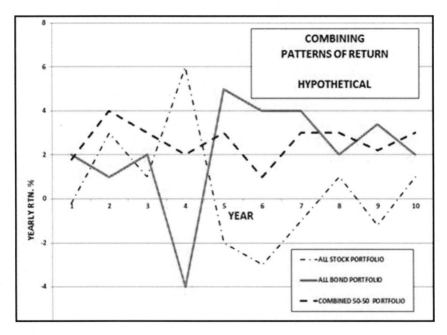

Note how the bond portfolio returns are out of phase with stock returns. Combining these two asset classes can result in a smoothed overall portfolio (dashed line, 50-50 bonds-stocks) return. We could go further and discuss the work of the Nobel laureates, but that's not why I wrote this book.

I'm here offering a much simpler way to approach and understand the market. My *theory of relativity* starts with table 5.1 below. This is a table from the *Ibbotson 2014 Yearbook*.[24] Ibbotson combined the stocks from the New York Stock Exchange (NYSE), the American Exchange, and the NASDAQ by market capitalization into one capitalization market set. He then divided this set into deciles and tracked performance of each decile from 1926 to the recent. The largest market cap stocks would go into the top decile rank (currently 176 companies equal to > $12 trillion total market cap). The next lower decile was filled, and so on. Currently, the lowest decile has 1,015 companies with total market cap of < $156 billion. Stocks growing or shrinking in market cap would move up or down in ranking at the end of each year. Deciles 1 and 2 are called large cap, 3–5 are midcaps, 6–8 are small caps, and 9–10 are microcaps.

The first thing that jumps out at you in table 5.1 is the almost linearity of returns as a function of size. Returns improve as we go smaller, and this is consistent with the data I showed you in chapter 1. In chapter 1, I stressed that we could relate fundamental parameters, such as price to book (value versus growth) to size. Now I want to tie it all together by suggesting that in a rough approximation, the bottoms of each decile category (smaller size) are value stocks, and the top of each category (larger size) are growth stocks. I've labeled the deciles (far right) to show what I mean.

Table 5.1. Long-term returns by decile (1926–2013)[24]

Decile	Geometric Mean Rtn	Arithmetic Mean Rtn.	Std. Dev.	Authors' Notation
Largest				
1	9.3 %	11.1 %	19.1%	growth
2	10.7	13.1	22.1	value
3	11.1	13.7	23.6	growth
4	11.1	14.1	25.8	
5	11.6	14.9	26.6	value
6	11.6	15.1	27.2	growth
7	11.6	15.5	29.4	
8	11.8	16.6	33.9	value
9	11.9	17.2	36.1	
10—smallest	13.4	20.9	45.4	
Mid cap 3–5	11.2	14.0	24.6	
Low cap 6–8	11.7	15.5	29.0	
Microcap 9–10	12.4	18.4	38.6	

Source: *Ibbotson SBBI 2014 Classic Yearbook*

Before and during my 48 years in the markets, there has been an almost infinite amount of research effort into stock picking by fundamental analysis. They range from *Security Analysis* by Graham-Dodd (1934) to more modern efforts by Ken Fisher (price-to-sales ratio) in *Super Stocks* (1984), Geraldine Weise (dividends) in *Dividends Don't Lie* (1988), and Peter Lynch (PEG ratio) in *Beating the Street* (1993). O'Shaughnessy, in *What Works on Wall Street*, pulled it all together by combining value (fundamental) factors (1996). All these authors made contributions to securities analysis, and most became quite affluent because of their work.

These authors had extensive data and performed thoughtful analysis. What I didn't know when I was reading these books was that they were all correct. All their fundamental approaches, in a broad sense, were correct but were leading me back to the smaller-size stocks. Let me explain with the help of table 5.2. Here, I'm using the most popular fundamental ratios, P/E, P/B, and dividend yield. I obtained these values from the fact sheets provided by the exchange-traded fund (ETF) vendor, iShares.[25] It's fairly straightforward from table 5.2 that if lower P/E or P/B ratios or higher dividend yields were driving your stock selection, then you would be driven to the value side (smaller cap) regardless of if you were looking in the small-, mid-, or large-cap category.

Over the years, these wonderful books were guiding me to smaller-market-cap-size stocks. *Returns are relative to size.* Ibbotson had been saying that for decades. Man has stirred the data pot until the market has become unrecognizable.

Table 5.2. Fundamental valuations and size (June 30, 2014)[25]

AS of 6/30/2014T		ISHARES TICKER	TRAILING P/E RATIO	TRAILING P/B RATIO	12 MOS TRAILING DIV. YLD.	
S&P 500	GROWTH	IVW	25.65	5.9	1.4	
	VALUE	IVE	19.29	3.08	2.08 ⬅ lower P/E, P/B Higher Div. Yld.	
S&P 400	GROWTH	IJK	28.92	4.860	.83	
	VALUE	IJJ	27.34	2.65	1.44 ⬅ lower P/E, P/B Higher Div. Yld.	
S&P 600	GROWTH	IJT	32.29	4.40	.69	
	VALUE	IJS	27.49	2.27	1.31 ⬅ ower P/E, P/B Higher Div. Yld.	

Data source: iShares.com

My *theory of relativity* is simplistic (and not original), to be sure. My contribution is to help you to understand how these seemingly conflicting (fundamental) approaches coalesce into a single unified idea. The authors above could and probably would say that their staff could come up with many overlooked larger-cap stocks in a given category that had the attributes of high-return small caps. Most likely though, you don't have a staff. With millions of computers out there, virtually nothing is overlooked. If you're very young, you don't have the time either. In addition to working 40–60 hours a week at a career, you're probably starting a family and you're told that you need to be reading and attending parenting skill classes. Oh, didn't we tell you? You should also be studying estate planning so that you will have enough money to retire someday. What if you die before retirement? Have you been studying various life and medical insurance options to make sure your young family is protected? Don't forget religion. Your church or synagogue needs you to volunteer your time. This is an excellent way for you and your family to demonstrate your faith. In other words, you've got to reduce the market down to its most simplistic elements in order for you to understand and cope with market dynamics. You simply don't have the time otherwise.

At this juncture in investment history, more and more of us are investing in international stocks. Wall Street is stirring the data pot again. They tell us not to try this at home but, rather, to let them utilize their vast expertise to aid us, for a fee, of course. They tell us they have people on the ground in Hong Kong, Bangkok, and Istanbul. They tell us they are meeting with CEOs, CFOs, and government officials and have private jets available to whisk them to whichever part of the world needs attention. They have teams (more overhead) available to study all the country-specific economic parameters. You can't do all these. You don't have to. For years, I have been tracking size performance of foreign stocks using the Standard & Poor's Broad Market Indices (BMI). Let's use this BMI data to take a trip around the world. The next few charts will look at size performance before, during, and after the 2008 financial crash. Figure 5.2 shows the 5-year total return for S&P value and growth indices for multiple regions and countries prior to 2008. A thoughtful glance shows that value outperformed growth around the world except in the commodity-driven Australian markets.

Figure 5.2. S&P BMI value and growth index total returns (July 2–July 7)[26]

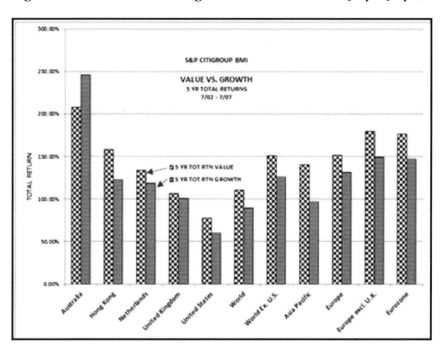

Source: S&P Dow Jones Indices LLC

If my theory were to hold that value and growth fundamentals direct you to size, then we would have expected smaller-cap stocks to have outperformed in these regions during the same period. Figure 5.3 shows the 5-year returns for small caps (< $1.5 billion) and large caps (> $5 billion) over the same period as in figure 5.2.

Figure 5.3. S&P BMI small and large cap index total returns (July 2–July 7)[26]

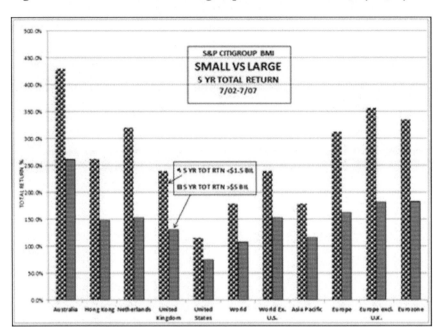

Data source: S&P Dow Jones Indices LLC

Indeed, small caps handily outperform their large-cap counterparts around the planet. This time, with no exceptions. It's interesting to note that small caps outperformed their fundamental brethren (value) 270% to 152% during the period. The difference in thinking size versus fundamentals was huge. Okay, let's move on to the crash of 2008. Figure 5.4 again shows stock performance around the planet during the crisis using our old friends value and growth.

Figure 5.4. S&P BMI value and growth index total returns[26]

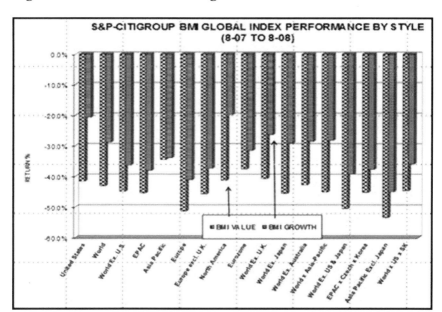

Data source: S&P Dow Jones Indices LLC

Value underperformed everywhere. Looking at size (figure 5.5), the theory holds. Small caps also underperformed around the planet. Value and growth were down on average –44.3% and –32.8% respectively. Small and large were down –45.7 and –32.8% on average. *Stocks move by size!* Let's move on.

Figure 5.5. S&P BMI size total returns (August 7–August 8)[26]

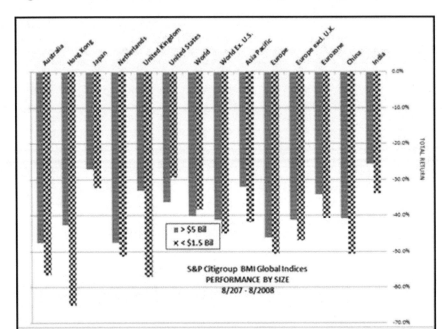

Data source: S&P Dow Jones Indices LLC

I will conclude my treatise with a current (August 5, 2014) look at 5-year returns after the financial crash. Figure 5.6 is a summary chart of 4 different categories of performance.

Figure 5.6. S&P BMI 5-year returns[26]

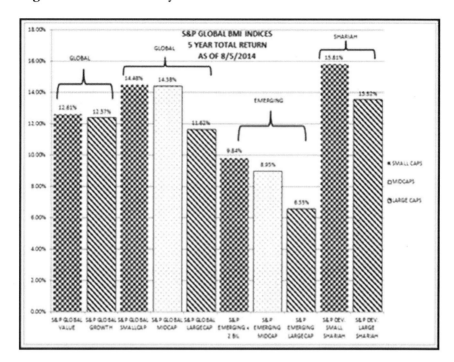

Data source: S&P Dow Jones Indices LLC

Moving left to right in figure 5.6, we see global performance for all value versus growth (12.6% versus 12.4%), global small versus global large (14.5% versus 14.4%), emerging small, mid, and large (9.8% versus 8.9% versus 6.6%), and finally, Shariah small versus Shariah large (15.8% versus 13.5%). That's incredible.

Think of the diversity of economies on this planet. There are capitalistic, socialistic, semicommunist, centrally planned, and not so centrally planned economies. Even using Shariah principles to select stocks, we got the same performance phenomena. Small outperformed large. *Stocks moved by size. Up and down.*

Your task, should you decide to take this mission, is to determine what size will outperform over your next holding period. How do you do that? Many good people have tried to figure this out and have published. Check out my bibliography, "Books That Made Me Think", on page 104. However, I think the solution comes through technical analysis (coming in the later chapters). We will get to that after I lay one more piece of foundation. That, my friend, is what I call the herd game.

The Chinese understand that when risk meets opportunity, You have Crisis!

CHAPTER SIX

It's a Herd Game

Herds Have Emotions Too

In the 1960s, I started chasing the stock market like a young wildebeest following the migrating herds on the Serengeti plains of Africa as depicted on the cover. Over the years, I observed that the herd went around and around the plains in a never-ending cycle, looking for better grass just over there (somewhere). Along the way, some of the daring young wildebeest would stray out to the fringes of the herd and were picked off by the lions (stockbrokers). The lions knew that the young wildebeest tasted good but didn't have large 401(k)s. Sometimes, they waited for the older wildebeest that weren't as tasty but had huge 401(k)s. As the herd proceeded, it needed water and had to wade into and across rivers where the silent alligators (mutual funds) lived. The alligators weren't discriminatory; they ate whatever came their way. Many of the herd survived by not taking chances—by staying in the middle, where the warmth of the herd kept them safe.

The herd migration was so regular that you could map and predict where the herd would be during the year (green patch on the cover). The predators lined up for each cycle. After years of going around in circles and eating dust, the older, slower wildebeest (the long-term investors) were exhausted and fell out of the protection of the herd and were pounced upon by the vultures (insurance companies). The vultures' task was to take what was left—of the 401(k)—on the bones and to shroud the carcass from the view of the herd with guaranteed protection plans (annuities). This is a cynical view of the markets, to be sure.

But it helps me explain the constantly moving yet repeatable nature of the markets in the raw terms of reality. I believe that the 1980s were a turning point for the US economy and the stock market. It was in the 1980s that the individual retirement accounts (IRA) and, eventually, the 401(k)s were sanctioned by the government and began to be implemented in mass. The government allowed tax deferred status on these accounts until the owner turned 59 ½. Many people (a lot of baby boomers) began to invest in stocks via these accounts for the first time. People bought mutual funds and, eventually, stock and bond indexes for both domestic and international stocks.

As a consequence of the many forms of IRAs and 401(k)s, people owned hundreds, if not a thousand, stocks. They no longer bought stocks because of some intrinsic fundamental value, as we discussed in the last chapter. They bought stocks by category. Their decisions were in part driven by what they had learned at the water cooler and what they had learned in the media. Television shows like *Wall Street Week with Louis Rukeyser* and the Financial News Network (predecessor to CNBC) came into vogue.

In general, shareholders weren't cognizant in real time if XYZ stock didn't make the numbers. They had no idea if CEO compensation was appropriate for company XYZ. In short, *the linkage between the owners of the company (shareholders) and the executive management team was severed.*

In the 1990s, I remember listening to a fund manager on CNBC. He commented that massive amounts of pension and 401(k) money came into his fund twice a month from large corporations. He said it was regular like a pulsing heartbeat. For him, the stock market game had reduced to moving massive money flows into and out of the market.

In the 1995–2000 bull market investors bought Intel stock based not on earnings but on the semiconductor book-to-bill ratios. Investors bought any stock related to personal computers or the Internet. And they bought large cap. The delta (difference) between large caps and small cap performance (5-year annualized) as measured by Ibbotson[22] for 1995–1999 was 10.07%, one of the highest 5-year deltas since World War II. From the same source (figure 6.1), the 10-year delta for 1990–1999 was 3.12%, the highest since WWII. Now I'm cherry-picking data here to tell a story.

Figure 6.1. 10-year holding period returns small versus large cap (annualized)[26]

Data source: S&P Dow Jones Indices LLC

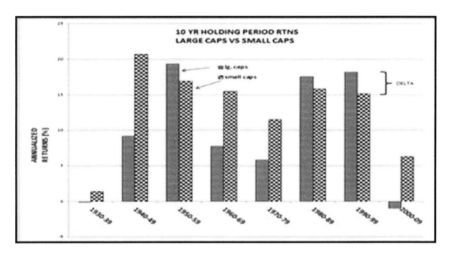

I'm telling you all this to convince you that the stock market game you're into is not your fathers' stock market. It's now about money constantly moving around the planet in a never-ending quasi-predictable cycle. It's about new money and old money. It's about careless money and cautious money—a lot of money (trillion dollars). *It moves by herd thinking.*

Let me show you how it works with the aid of figure 6.2. Stock prices are the solid rising black line. The size of the large arrows represents the amount of money coming into the market. At a stock market bottom (bottom left), few people think that stocks can go up and don't buy. However, there are wise (and lucky) investors that decide to nibble and do buy. The market comes off the bottom, and the nibblers were correct (stocks are going up). They tell their friends and colleagues, and some of those decide to nibble with a little discretionary money, and indeed, they are also correct (stocks are going up). The word starts to get out via the media that stocks are at a multiyear high. More money comes in off the sidelines as people rationalize that the previous economic calamity has been solved and not likely to return. Since the bottom, everyone has been right (stocks are going up).

As you get closer and closer to the top, the media informs the public that stocks have been going up for years now and that records are being broken.

Experts come onto financial television and inform the public as to how they have made great sums of money for their clients.

Figure 6.2. Herd behavior and the market

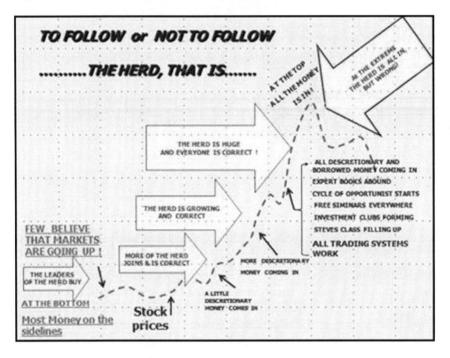

Everyone is correct (stocks are going up). The cycle of opportunist starts (experts pop up everywhere). Books start hitting the shelves on how easy it is to make money in the markets. Investment clubs double and triple in attendance. My classes also double and triple in size. Free trading seminars seem to be happening every week.

Amazingly, almost every trading system seems to make money. *Everyone is correct (stocks are going up).*

"Why does he keep saying everyone is correct?" you ask? At some point in this time line, books about being a contrarian investor will proliferate. They appeal to your ego, suggesting that thinking independently of the herd results in better returns. I want you to realize that going against the herd all the way up would have been disastrous. The herd was right, stocks were going up. *It's at the top (the extreme) that the herd is wrong.* I tell people in class that it's when you see the tails of the wildebeest in front of you go straight up, that you want to leave the herd. Straight up means veer left or right, they just went over the cliff.

So how do you know when the market is at the top? You can't know until it's past. *But you can tell when a market is near an extreme.* This brings up a point I try to bring out in every class.

No one can predict the future; however, *knowing where you are in the market can still make you a lot of money.* Our primary tool for analyzing market extremes is technical analysis. However, this chapter is about herd behavior, and I want to close on observing herd behavior. Figure 6.3 is a wonderful little chart describing the emotions of the participants as they go through a bull market, followed by a bear market, and followed by a new bull and so on.

When you go to a cocktail or business party, listen for the general conversation of the group. If they are talking stocks, listen for how easy or how tough it is to make money. Try to figure out where the group is on the sine wave in figure 6.3. You can also use and take advantage of the media for clues for where you are in the cycle.

Figure 6.3. Market Cycle of Emotions

THE STOCK MARKET
CYCLE OF EMOTIONS

EUPHORIA ,
I'M QUITTING MY DAY JOB !

THIS IS EASY !

ANXIETY:
IT WILL COME BACK

EXCITEMENT

OPTIMISM

FEAR & DENIAL :
I'M A LONG TERM
INVESTOR ANYWAY

DESPERATION

OPTIMISM

IT WAS MY BROKERS FAULT :
I KNOW IT WAS GOING DOWN

LETS TRY REAL ESTATE :
THERE NOT MAKING ANY MORE

CASH ME OUT

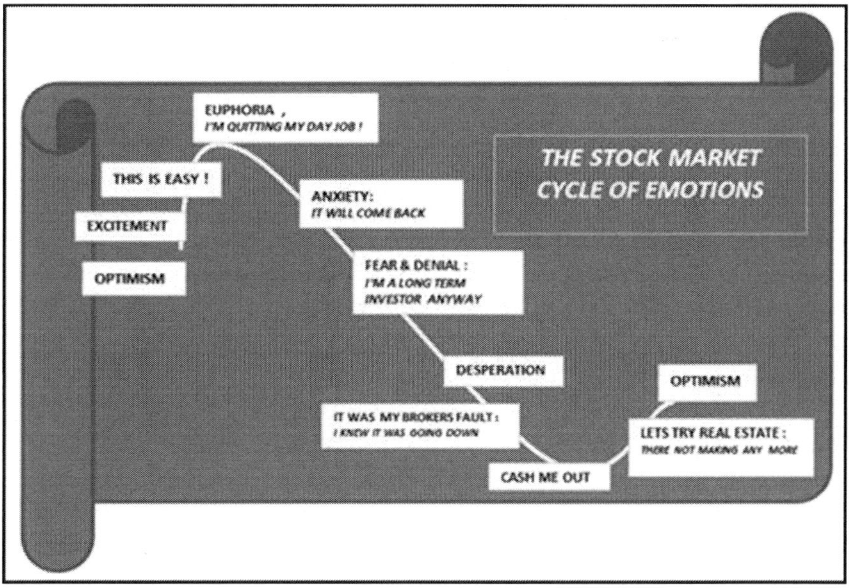

Realize that the media is constantly polling the herd to find out if it (the herd) is scared or enthusiastic about some economic item or event driving the markets. The media then reinforces that emotion by supplying even more information. This informs the reader that they (the media) are on top of it.

Finally, the media will advise the reader to stay tuned or read tomorrow's journal article since they have access to experts that will advise the reader what needs to be done to survive or take advantage of the current situation. The media's job is to sell the media, not to make you money. *Use the media to give you clues as to where the herd's emotions lie.*

Another anecdotal form of herd analysis using the media is to scan book titles after a major market downturn. For example, I bought the books *How to Beat the Depression That Is Surely Coming* by R. Persons, PhD; *Crisis Investing: Opportunities in the Coming Great Depression* by D. Casey; and *Financial Reckoning Day: Surviving the Soft Depression of the 21st Century* by W. Bonner and A. Wiggin. The first book was published after the 1974 market crash; the second (published in 1979), after the turbulent inflation and stock price stagnation of the seventies. The last book was published in 2003 after the Internet bubble burst. Even Joseph Granville (inventor of on-balance volume) predicted a crash as inevitable in his book *The Warning: The Coming Great Crash in the Stock Market* (published in 1985). As you can see by the publishing date, some of these authors have been waiting for decades to be right. I believe, these crash books are really telling you the stock market bottom is in and most of the money is out.

Today we have authors who go both ways. We have H. Dent, my favorite opportunist, publishing *The Roaring 2000s: Building the Wealth and Lifestyle You Desire in the Greatest Boom in History,* in which he predicted a Dow Jones price of 21,500 to 35,000 by the year 2008 (published in 1998). After the crash of 2008, Harry Dent went the other way. In 2009, he published *The Great Depression Ahead: How to Prosper in the Debt Crisis of 2010–2012* (published in 2009). He also wrote *The Great Crash Ahead* (published in 2012), predicting a crash sometime between mid-2012 and early 2015. Or how about his book entitled *The Next Great Bubble Boom: How to Profit from the Greatest Boom in History: 2006–2010* (published in 2006)?

I stopped buying these books years ago. These authors make similar mistakes but not always the same mistake. They believe that they have discovered an economic fault line that only they can see and interpret, that the government is blind or full of incompetents or there is a grand conspiracy in the government to sink the world economy so that the very rich can obtain control.

The other grand mistake these authors make is the assumption that their scenario of doom and catastrophe is inevitable, that man is incapable of changing his economic path once he is on it. That's silly. You only have to follow the Federal Reserve for the last few decades to have witnessed tremendous zigzags in policy to head off catastrophe. Besides, man is ingenious at digging himself out of the very same hole he just put himself into.

I hope these soothsayers mean well. They certainly make a ton of money writing these books. In 47 years, I've yet to make any money from their advice.

The media uses the herd's emotions to sell the media. You can use the media to understand the herd's emotions and whether the emotions are at an extreme. It's at the extreme when the herd is wrong.

Let's summarize this chapter. As an investor, your job is to monitor the direction and emotion of the herd, enjoy the grass, keep an eye out for lions and alligators, stay alive, and watch the tail in front of you. Remember . . .

> **ALWAYS DRINK UPSTREAM**
>
> **FROM THE HERD!**

What have we learned so far? The stock market game is no longer about picking a stock; it's about picking asset classes or groups.

History tells us that the best performing groups have been best understood by size (small beat large). Fundamental analysis of balance sheets and financial statements does work but tends to pull us back to size. So stay with the simplicity of size as a tool to understand and manage your stock market investments.

Learn to filter data. Almost all important data is sourced from the government. It is then disseminated and sometimes spun by the press and media. Learn about the data being reported so that you can draw your own conclusions. As President Reagan once said, "Trust but verify." Remember the old western movies when one night, the chuck wagon cook dropped the frying pans and set off a stampede in the herd. Learn to step aside as the herd stampedes to the latest headlines. *Don't let the news do that to you.*

It's a herd game, and you have to learn herd dynamics if you are to survive. As if all these weren't enough, you must keep an eye on the predators that follow the herd. They offer quick and easy solutions to finding greener grass and abundant water. Sometimes, their offers even come with guarantees. But who guarantees them? Let me close with a few lines from the Desiderata by Max Ehrmann.

> EXERCISE CAUTION IN YOUR BUSINESS AFFAIRS FOR THE WORLD IS FULL OF TRICKERY.
>
> BUT LET THIS NOT BLIND YOU TO WHAT VIRTUE THERE IS: MANY PERSONS STRIVE FOR HIGH IDEALS. AND EVERYWHERE LIFE IS FULL OF HEROISM.

CHAPTER SEVEN

Monitoring the Herd Part I

There's More Than One Herd

Okay, it's a herd game. How do we monitor the herd? Fortunately, we have a lot of tools to do just that. Let's start with the University of Michigan consumer sentiment survey. You can get the University of Michigan survey results at the St. Louis Federal Reserve site in the Fred database. I'm showing it in figure 7.1.[27] The data spans from 1952 to 2011. The average reading is 85 (horizontal line). I've identified sentiment tops with circles. I've identified some market crashes and market bottoms (arrows). The star at the far right is the current reading at the time of this writing.

You can see that market tops are usually preceded or coincident with exuberance and market bottoms are preceded or are coincident with consumer negativism. Sentiment tends to *follow* the market higher or lower. *It's only at the extreme that you can derive predictive power from the herd. Remember, it's at the extreme when the herd is wrong.* You won't know if you're at a top or a bottom, but you can tell if you're at or in a range that preceded a top or bottom in the past. History has value.

Figure 7.1. Herd sentiment (University of Michigan sentiment survey)[27]

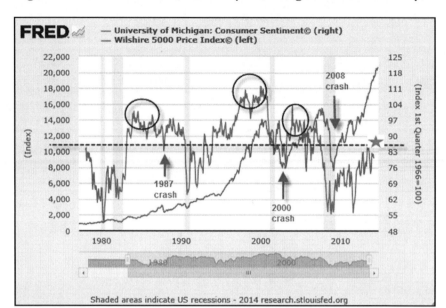

Source: FRED, Federal Reserve Bank of St. Louis, University of Michigan (with permission)

Another great way to monitor the herd is to watch what they are doing with their money. Talk is cheap, but where people actually put their money tells you something. Take a look at figure 7.2.

This is data from the Investment Company Institute (ICI), and the charts are from StockCharts.com.

Figure 7.2. Cash flows to stock and bond mutual funds (ICI data)

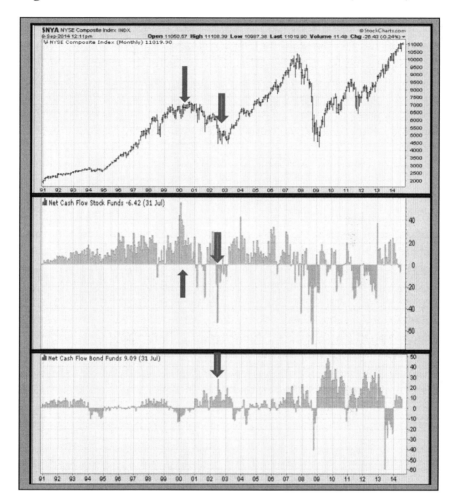

Source: StockCharts.Com

The top graph in figure 7.2 is the New York Composite Price Index from 1991 through September 8, 2014. The second graphic down is the cash flow into (up bars) and out of (down bars) stock mutual funds over the same period. The third graphic down is the cash flow into and out of bond mutual funds.

The arrows at the far left show the market action culminating at the 2000 market top. Note the stock buying and the bond selling as we approached the top. This is the classic buy-high (stocks), sell-low (bonds). The next set of arrows (right side) shows the typical stock market bottom during 2002–2003. Investors sold low (stocks) and bought high (bonds). The cycle is summarized as most of the buying was at the top; most of the selling was at the bottom for both markets. This herd behavior is in accordance with my description at the beginning of chapter 6. More and more people bought as the market went up. And the buyers were correct—the market was going up. They didn't know in 2000, the top was in.

But there were clues the top was near. Let's continue.

One of my most powerful tools for monitoring the herd is sideline money. By now you know that money leaves the market at bottoms. Where does it go? Yes, some of it goes to the bond market and can come back. New monies are being made from profits all the time. Where is it stored? I monitor two types of highly liquid money. The first is MZM (zero maturity money) and is primarily monies in checking accounts, savings, money markets, and cash in circulation. The other supply of money is Foreign Official Dollar Reserves (FRODOR) held by the US Federal Reserve for foreign entities, like the World Bank or the International Monetary Fund. All these monies are available to go into the market or anywhere else, for that matter. What's important is to know that it's out there. You can find MZM data in FRED. FRODOR is found in series H.4.1 at the Federal Reserve website. I sum these two items and plot them (figure 7.3) as a function (%) of the size of the US market. I use the Wilshire 5000 as my proxy for the market.

Figure 7.3. Sideline money and Wilshire 5000[28]

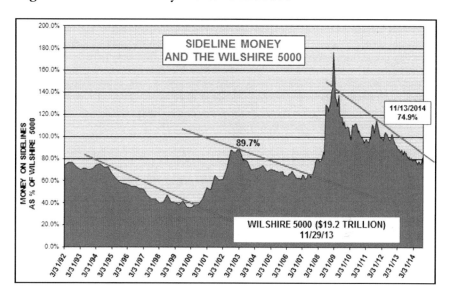

Data source: FRED, St. Louis Federal Reserve Bank

My data starts in 1992, and the amount of sideline money was about 78% the size of the market. As the great bull market of 1995–2000 commenced, money began leaving the sideline and moved into the stock market. Money flowed steadily as everyone began to think that stocks go up forever. At the peak of the market (2000), speculation was rampant and only 38% of sideline money was left (most of the money was in). Suddenly, the party was over, the Internet bubble burst, and money fled the scene and went back to the sidelines for safety. Everyone then believed that stocks go down forever.

The bull market reignited in March of 2003 with sideline money at about 90% (most of the money was out). Many people had moved to real estate, knowing that they're not making any more of it, knowing that real estate always goes up. Nevertheless, money began moving back into the market in 2003 and kept coming until the financial crash of 2008.

In 2008, the experts warned us that the world as we knew it was coming to an end. Investors piled out of stocks and into MZM components big-time. The experts warned of rampant inflation ahead, and investors bought gold. Sideline money peaked at almost 180% the size of the market. Not only was all the money out, but it was never coming back! Never!

As you can see from figure 7.3, the money did come back. It came back huge. From the March 2009 bottom, stocks have essentially tripled, and gold has made a round-trip from about $1,000 per ounce (April 2008) to $1,900 (September 2012) and back to $1,196 at this juncture. Today, yesterday, rampant inflation forgot to show up.

Yes, many things drive stock prices higher. As an engineer, I see sideline money as potential energy—potential energy ready to be converted to the kinetic energy of price movement. There are more sources of money. That's next.

When investors are very confident that stocks are going up, they will borrow money (leverage up) to buy stocks. We can monitor this herd of speculators by tracking borrowing (margin debt) levels on the New York Stock Exchange (NYSE). Fortunately, this data is provided for free by the exchange.[29] I've plotted it in figure 7.4.

The solid area in figure 7.4 is the Wilshire 5000 index, and again, I'm using it as a proxy for the market. The dotted line is the margin levels in billion dollars. The boxes give the margin amount and percentage as a size of the market. Notice the exponential surge in margin going into the 1999–2000 top and similarly in 2007. Going into 1999, margin levels were running a steady 1.2–1.3%, the size of the Wilshire 5000. They ran up to 1.9% in just a couple of months. This was a heads-up that investors were feeling quite confident and leveraging up to buy those stocks that they knew would always go up.

As you can see in figure 7.4, margin levels are getting high again. Not quite as high as the 2007 top but greater than the 2000 top. Although levels are high, when you normalize this level to the amount of highly liquid money in the system (MZM), they appear sustainable. I've done this for you in figure 7.5a.

Figure 7.4. Margin levels on NYSE[29]

Data source: NYSE and FINRA © 2015 FINRA. All rights reserved.

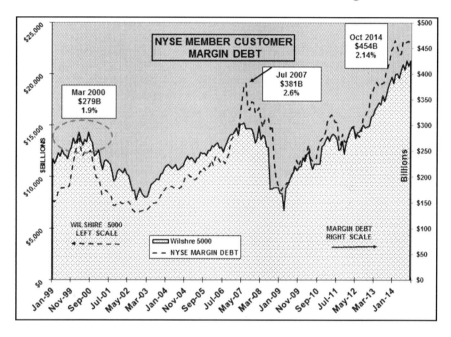

Understanding how much money is in the system provides you with context. Understanding where you are in the grand scheme of things is worth a fortune. But be careful when you see charts like 7.5a. They are great rationalizations for why the markets can go higher. Don't let them lull you to sleep. Stocks can continue higher, but if the Fed begins to pull money out of the system, MZM can slow, sending the ratio higher quickly. I think an excellent way to monitor margin debt is to look at how quickly it is growing relative to how fast stocks are rising.

I've plotted this for you in figure 7.5b.

Figure 7.5a. NYSE margin levels[29] normalized by MZM[28]

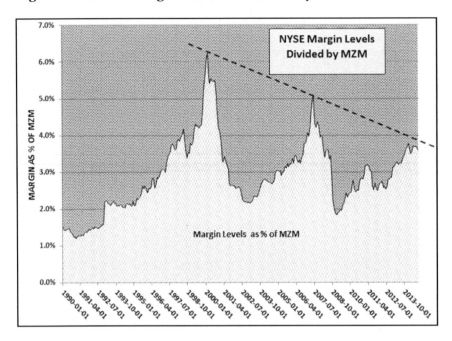

Figure 7.5b. NYSE margin levels and Wilshire 5000 (rate of change)

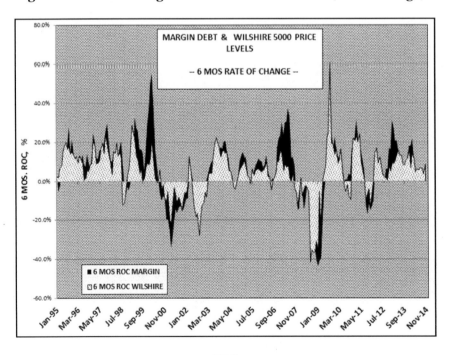

Figure 7.5b is a graph of the 6-month rate of change (ROC) of NYSE margin (solid black) with the 6-month ROC of the Wilshire 5000, superimposed in front. Notice the timing and the magnitude of change in the margin levels versus the Wilshire. The timing appears random, but focus on the magnitudes. There are areas where the margin level rates of change were huge compared to those of the market. These were at the top in 2000 and 2007. These data, these charts, look great as timing tools in hindsight. However, in real time, you don't know when the correction is coming. The market can go on for months in these extreme conditions before correcting. Therefore, they can't be used as exact timing tools. However, this type of data warns you that risk is rising. It also alerts you that risk has been wrung out as shown in 2001–2002 and 2009. The longer the condition exists, the greater or lesser the risk. Keep an eye on margin debt. It's a valuable part of the context.

So when does that money in FRODOR come in? you ask. Figure 7.6 is a short history (1994–2014) of foreign purchases (including foreign official) of US stocks. You can get this data from the Treasury International Capital system[30] website for free. The volatile dotted line is the monthly purchases of US stocks. The solid line is the six-month moving average of the monthly purchases. Notice the almost exponential rise in foreign purchases of US stocks as we moved into 2000. The six-month moving average peaked in March 2000, and the selling climax bottomed in August 2004. There was another surge in 2007 just before the financial crash. There can be more than one herd to watch, but they will all have similar behaviors. They buy more at the high and sell more at the low.

Figure 7.6. Foreign purchase of US stocks[30]

Data source: TIC

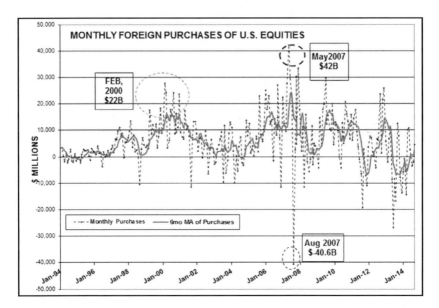

Data source: Treasury International Capital system

Before we move on to some really good stuff, let's pause and think a moment. I'm telling you that markets move by herd thinking. Knowing where the money is, how much is out there, and where it is coming from gives you clues about what the herd is thinking. It also gives clues as to the potential for the market to go higher (money is all out) or lower (money is all in). However, money levels and flows are not timing tools but indicators of sentiment and risk levels.

As you now know, markets run in states of extreme for months and years. You won't know the top is in until it's past, but you don't have to. There is nothing that says you have to hit the top or bottom perfectly. As an investor, you can dollar average in and out as you sense the action is getting a little too frothy. You can adjust your profit expectations and durations if you're a trader.

DON'T CONFUSE BRAINS WITH A BULL MARKET!

CHAPTER EIGHT

Monitoring the Herd Part II

Keeping an Eye on the Leader

We said in chapter 4 that stocks move in anticipation of monetary policy. This is called Fed watch. One of the ways we do this is to watch interest rates. More specifically, we watch the yield curve. The *yield curve is defined as the term structure of interest rates*,[31] and the current curve is shown in figure 8.1.

Figure 8.1. US treasury yield curve[31]

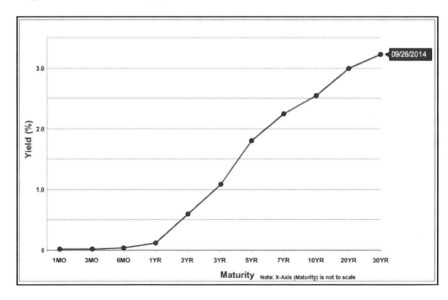

Data source: US Department of Treasury

The yield curve shows the cost of borrowing over a given time frame or maturity. Since the US government is considered the safest investment in the country, then all other forms of credit should be derived off this curve. *The Fed has traditionally manipulated the short end (short duration) of the curve* to steepen the curve (stimulate economic growth), which is shown in figure 8.2.

Figure 8.2. Steep yield curves[31]

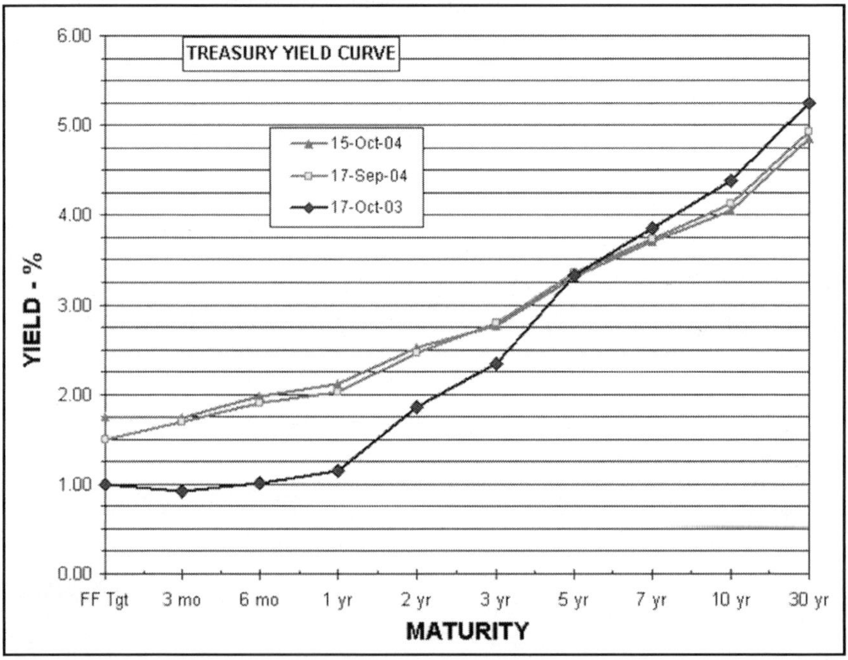

Data source: US Department of Treasury

Likewise, the Fed can raise the front end of the curve (slow economic growth) until short rates equal long rates as in a flat curve (bottom curve in figure 8.3). Or the Fed can continue tightening until short rates are higher than long rates and the curve is said to be inverted.

Figure 8.3. Flat and inverted yield curves[31]

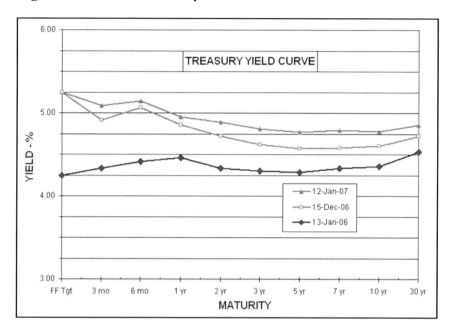

Data source: US Department of Treasury

By raising or lowering the yield curve, the Fed is raising or lowering the cost of borrowing money. Individuals and companies will hold off borrowing when they perceive marginal economic conditions lie ahead. *Rising interest rates signal marginal conditions ahead or at least that the Fed is driving in that direction.*

Let's see what happened to interest rates during the bull market cycle of 1995–2000. Figure 8.4 shows the yield curves at three points in time from 1995 to 1997. To help you visualize the shape, I've calculated the difference (delta) between the long end (30-year bond) and the short end (3 months T-bill) and put the numbers below each graph. Note the deltas were all positive and ranged from 0.77 to 1.98%.

Note what happened as the bull market aged into 1998–2000 (figure 8.5). The Fed began to shift the front end of the curve upward, and the deltas shrank until going negative in May of 2000. The bull market peaked in March of 2000. Remember, watching the Fed and other central bank policies is crucial to understanding investment context. The yield curve is a direct link into the minds of the policy makers. So how does the Fed move the front end of the curve? They do that with the federal funds rate.

Figure 8.4. Yield curves (1995–1997)[31]

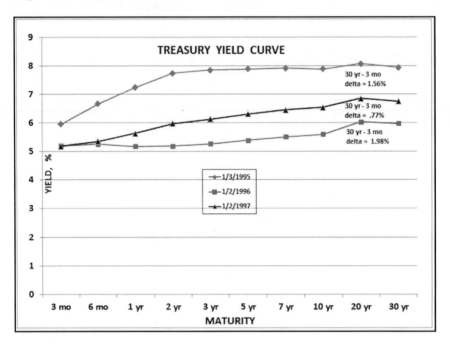

Source: US Department of Treasury

Figure 8.5. Yield curves 1998–2000[31]

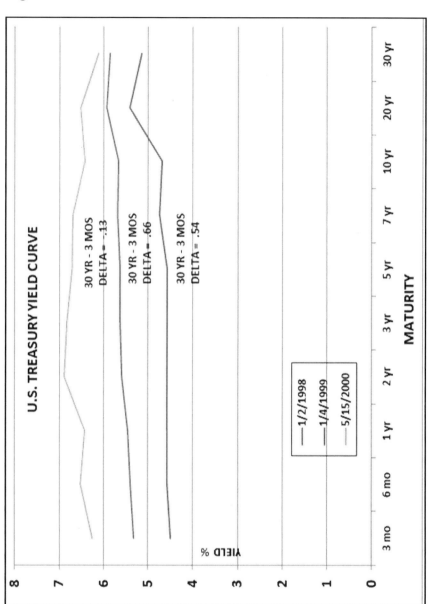

Source: US Department of Treasury

As we discussed in chapter 4, banks maintain deposits at the Federal Reserve to meet reserve requirements. If they have excess reserves, they can lend the excess to other banks that don't have enough reserves at the federal funds rate. *Effectively, the federal funds rate sets the floor for short-term interest rates.* Figure 8.6 shows how the two rates have tracked since 1968.

Figure 8.6. Federal funds rate and 3 months T-bill (1968–2014)[32]

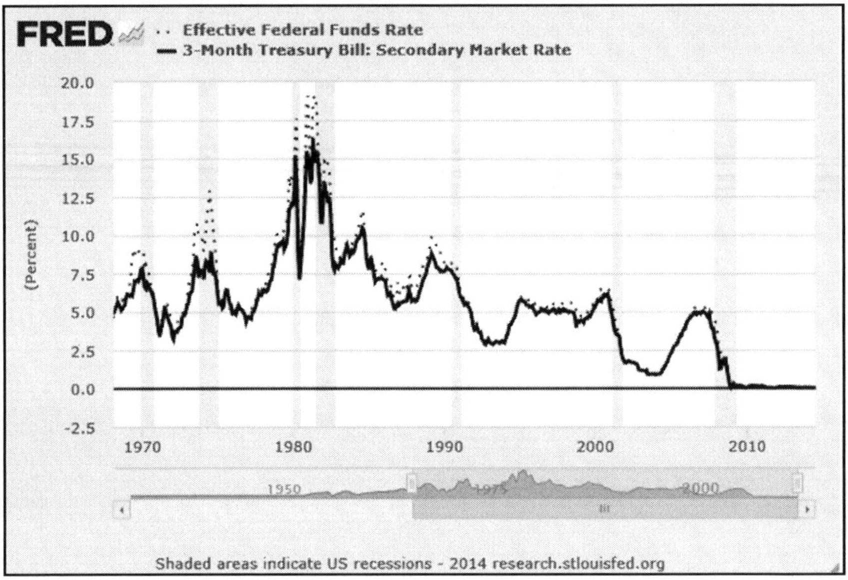

FRED ·· Effective Federal Funds Rate
— 3-Month Treasury Bill: Secondary Market Rate

Shaded areas indicate US recessions - 2014 research.stlouisfed.org

Source: FRED, Federal Reserve Bank of St. Louis

So the Fed moves the front end of the yield curve, changing the cost of money as one of its tools to stimulate or put a drag on the US economy. As we approached the market top in 2000, the herd was not watching what it should have been. The herd was focused on how fast the profits were coming. Watching the yield curve isn't watching the herd directly; rather, it's observing if the herd is running toward a cliff. It's observing if risk is changing. The herd was wrong at the top—the extreme. You must keep an eye on the Fed and yield curve for signals that monetary policy is shifting. The markets will eventually detect this shift and react accordingly.

WRONG IS WRONG !
EVEN IF EVERYONE IS DOING IT

RIGHT IS RIGHT !
EVEN IF ONLY YOU ARE DOING IT !

CHAPTER NINE

Monitoring the Herd Part III

Measuring the Vitals of the Market with Technical
Analysis Using the McClellan Summation

We all tend to watch the price action of the markets to keep score.

However, *we need to keep track of the health of the market.* We need to know if the internals are solid or are weakening. This is called breadth analysis. My favorite tool for doing this is the McClellan Summation. This wonderful indicator was developed by Sherman and Marian McClellan in the 1960s and is in widespread use today.

The summation is a modified advance-decline line. Each day, you would count the number of advancing stocks (closed higher than yesterday) and declining stocks (closed lower than yesterday) of the index you're tracking. Create a 19-day and 39-day exponential moving average (EMA) of the difference between advances and decliners. Subtract the 19-day EMA from the 39-day EMA, and you have the McClellan Oscillator. Add today's oscillator to the summation of all previous oscillator values, and you have the McClellan Summation. Sounds very messy, and it is. But you have available technical analysis software that does it all for you. So it ends up being easy. Let's go to figure 9.1 to see how easy.

The upper graphic in figure 9.1 is the Dow Jones Industrial Average (DJIA) from 1967 to 1981, and I've circle some nasty drops. Notice the circles in the chart below the DJIA line up. I've also placed a horizontal line at about –1500 (right scale) on the second chart.

Figure 9.1. McClellan Summation (DJIA)

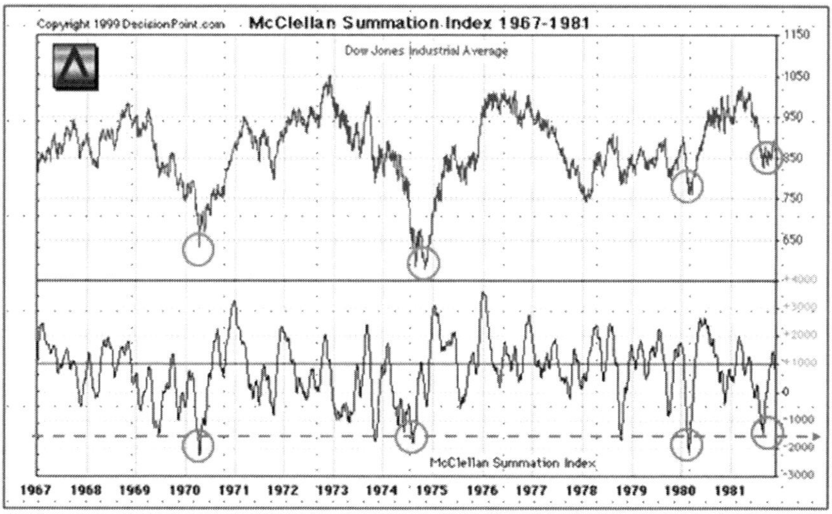

Source: StockCharts.com

The summation tends to form sharp downward spikes at market bottoms in the range of about –1500 for the DJIA. This tool is excellent for helping you identify market bottoms. That's when you need it most. That's when you're the most afraid. Let's keep going. Figure 9.2 takes us forward in time, and we're using a larger index, the NYSE Composite. Again, we see some pretty sharp spikes in the McClellan Summation around the –1500 line at the composite bottoms.

Figure 9.2. NYSE Composite Index

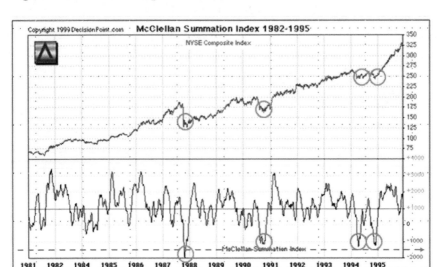

Source: StockCharts.com

These two charts demonstrate how the summation acts as a confirming indicator. *It confirms the bottoming action.* There is much more that could be said about its confirmation characteristics, but I want to spend most of my time here on its leading indicator value. This is the bread and butter of its worth.

In 1987, we underwent a pretty severe market crash in October. Figure 9.3 (top graph) shows the NYSE Composite reaching a bottom in October and then a lower low reached (arrow) in the December time frame. The McClellan Summation (center graph) also hit low around –1500 in October. Notice that on the second lower low for the composite, we had a higher low (arrow) for the summation. This was telling us that the market internals were getting stronger. The composite was stronger at the second low than at the first low. *The healing process had begun.* The McClellan Summation is acting as a leading indicator in this instance. The market had 3–4 more years of a bull run left in it.

Figure 9.3. McClellan Summation and 1987 crash

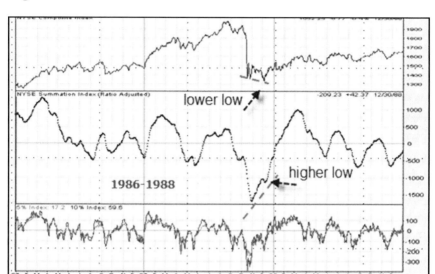

Source: StockCharts.com

Let's keep moving forward in time. How about the 1998 debacle (figure 9.4)?

Figure 9.4. McClellan Summation and 1998 crash

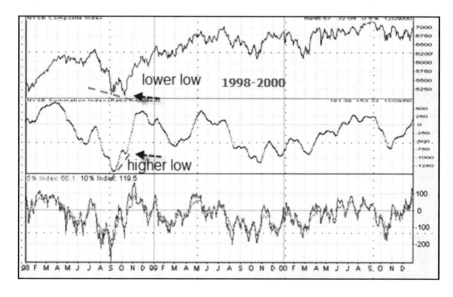

Source: StockCharts.com

The composite hit bottom around –1400 (sound familiar?) in September, followed by a lower low in November. The McClellan Summation puts in a low in September with a higher low in November. *The summation was again acting as a leading indicator telling us that the market was healing internally and the bottom was in.* We had another 18 months of price increases ahead of us. We've demonstrated how well the summation does as a confirming and leading indicator of bottoms. How does it do with finding tops?

Figure 9.5 is the NYSE Composite from 1996 to 2002. Here's what happened. The McClellan Summation peaked near July 1997 (point *O*) and put in a series of successive lower tops that I have labeled *A, B, C,* etc. The market, as measured here, continued higher as the summation dropped. Note that point *A* on the summation corresponds to point *A* on the composite and they both occurred just before the market rolled over for the 1998 Long-Term Capital Management hedge fund debacle correction in May.

Notice that as the market climbed higher and higher, each successive peak in the summation was lower than our starting point at *O*. I hope the utility of the summation is evident here. Each successive lower peaked warned of an impending intermediate term correction—some large; some small. In addition, the long sequence of lower tops in the summation but higher tops in the composite was warning that the bull market was losing strength. The index was reaching new highs, but less and less of the underlying stocks were participating in the advance.

Figure 9.5. McClellan Summation and NYSE Composite (1996–2002)

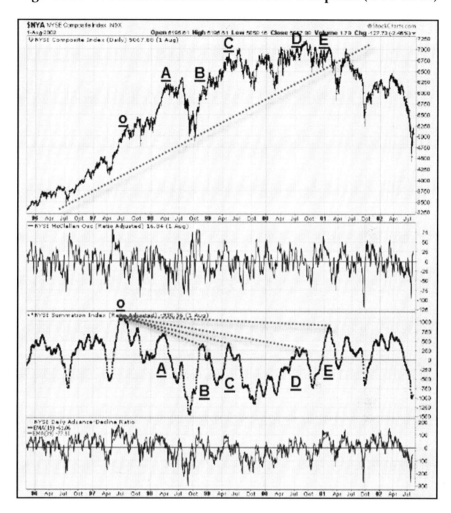

Source: StockCharts.com

You now have a feel for how well the summation identifies topping action. The problem, as you may have discerned, is that topping action can be sharp as in the case of the intermediate term corrections we've just described. Topping action can also be agonizingly slow. The summation began warning of weakness in the markets as early as 1997–1998, but the final top wasn't in until 2000. However, each successive lower peak was telling us to become more conservative, more defensive. *In short, each lower peak in the summation was telling us that risk was rising.*

IN THE MARKETS, YOU CAN'T PREDICT THE FUTURE

BUT, KNOWING WHERE YOU ARE TODAY CAN BE WORTH A FORTUNE !

CHAPTER TEN

Monitoring the Herd Part IV

Measuring the Vitals of the Market with
Technical Analysis Using Money Flow

Another great tool to complement the summation is my favorite indicator—
the *Money Flow Index* (MFI). This indicator is included in almost all
technical analysis software today. It measures the strength of money flowing
in and out of a security. The working hypothesis is that price movement
is confirmed and sometimes led by the money moving ahead of the news.
Money flow is a measure of conviction of the price move. It is a combined price
and volume indicator that presents as an oscillator moving between 0 and
100%. Two horizontal lines are usually drawn at 20% (oversold) and 80%
(overbought). The calculation of MFI is straightforward and given by the
following:

Typical price = today (open + close + last) / 3

If today's typical price is higher than yesterday's typical price, then multiply
by today's volume and add to positive money flow column. If today's typical
is less than yesterday's, then multiply by today's volume and add to negative
money flow column. Ratio the sum of the two columns over the look-back
(LB) period of interest.

Money Flow ratio $_{(LB)}$ = (pos. money flow /neg. money flow) $_{(LB)}$

Money Flow Index $_{(LB)}$ = 100 – (100 / (1 + money flow ratio $_{(LB)}$)

A typical price chart with MFI is shown below in figure 10.1. I'm using a 13-day (bottom) and 21-day MFI (middle). Notice that EWW was declining from February 2014 till late March (declining trend line). During the same period, the MFI was rising as shown by the two rising trend lines I've drawn in the bottom two graphs. As the stock dropped, money began moving in. Finally, enough money came in to start driving the stock price upward as we saw from late March to early April.

Figure 10.1. Mexico ETF (EWW) and Money Flow Index

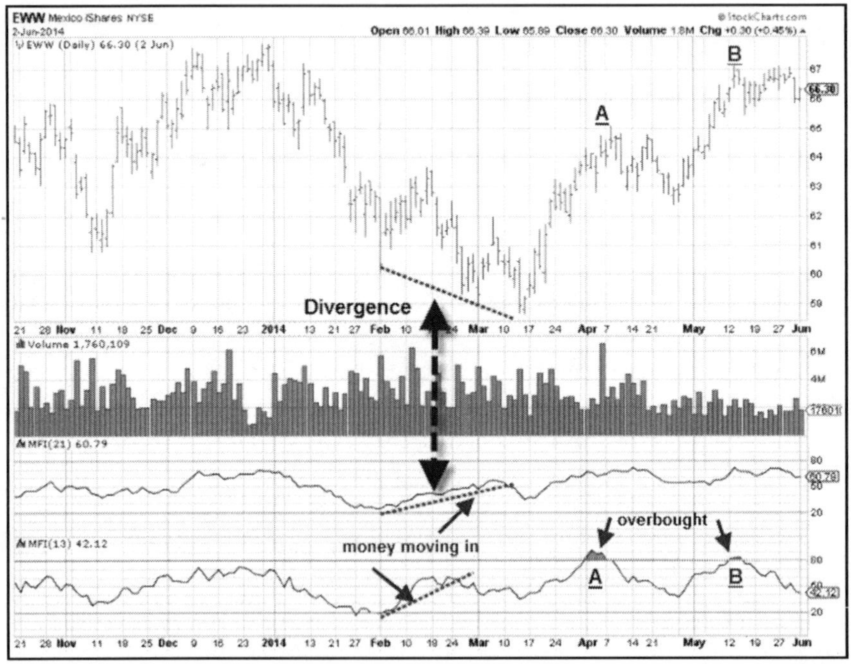

Source: StockCharts.com

This *setup of declining price and rising MFI is known as divergence.* In mid-March, the stock hit bottom and turned upward. Now the price and MFI moved in lockstep and MFI was confirming the price trend. MFI and price increased to point A where the MFI reached the overbought zone (> 80). The overbought region warns that the amount of money entering the stock is unsustainable. Indeed, point A was a short-term top. This cycle repeated itself at point B, another short-term top. Figure 10.2 shows a different variation on divergence and makes use of the oversold line at MFI ≤ 20.

Figure 10.2. Emerging markets ETF (EWX) and Money Flow Index

Source: StockCharts.com

In this case, MFI on the emerging markets ETF peaked in late June and stayed overbought till mid-July. The stock oscillated until reaching a new high in mid-September. However, the MFI diverged and failed to confirm the new price high in September. The stock rolled over and followed the MFI downward until reaching oversold (< 20) in late September. The oversold condition was relieved by a short-term rally into October. No new money came into the stock after the rally, and the stock then continued its downward plunge.

These two examples show the power of MFI. I use it as a *trend confirmation tool*. It gives you short-term oversold and overbought clip levels (< 20 and > 80). Combine this indicator with the McClellan Summation, and you have two of the most powerful indicators of trend strength ever. But!

There is always a but. I have to close this chapter with a short comment. Both the summation and MFI have one weakness, and I'm not sure the weakness is in the indicators or in the humans that use them. That weakness is *neither tells you when or why.* When you see divergence or an overbought/oversold condition, you still don't know when the price will reverse that condition. Sometimes this can go on for days, weeks, or months. It can take a great deal of patience to hang in there waiting for price confirmation or reversal. With time and experience, you will grow to trust these tools and develop judgment as to timing. Trust me. As to why, you may never know why. Stocks move on news and sometimes in anticipation of news.

Technical indicators tell you when a stock(s) has reached an extreme. They let you see distribution and accumulation in real time. If you're lucky, you may see a news release that explains why a stock moved up/down last month. Sometimes, the move is insider trading. People do cheat. Sometimes, it was a hedge fund taking a 5% position, and it filled out a SEC 13D form the following month. Sometimes, money leaves a stock knowing of a pending merger that is going to fall through. You may never read about this in the newspaper. *Use the technicals to tell you the reality on the ground now and take action.* Later, finding out why is nice but probably too late to make money on it.

CHAPTER ELEVEN

Mutual Funds or Indexes

It's Not Smoke. It's Haze!

When I first became a stockbroker, I was directed to a senior broker's office for training. The plate next to his door said he was a vice president. I was excited. Now I was going to learn something. He handed me a brochure from a family of mutual funds and told me to sprinkle new client money across any five funds in the brochure. He bid me good day. My training was over.

Over the next few years, I developed investment strategies that, based on index performance, were quite reasonable and I thought were good. However, my stock mutual fund picks (and therefore my strategies) never seem to perform as expected. My clients held me responsible since I had recommended the strategy and the mutual funds. This was a tremendous source of frustration for me. If only I could invest in the indexes, I would say to myself.

In 2000, iShares came out with a large set of exchange traded funds (ETF) that were designed to track market capitalization and style indices as managed by Standard & Poor's Corp. For the first time in my experience, I could take advantage of the data and ideas collected in the 20th century by Ibbotson and others. That year, I jumped ship to ETFs and never looked back.

As the Internet evolved, more and more information became available. In parallel, as indexing using ETFs became popular, more information about mutual fund performance became available on the Internet. Standard & Poor's now publishes a report on the web called Standard & Poor's Indices versus Active Managers (SPIVA) report.[33] It measures a sampling of actively managed mutual funds and their performance against their relevant S&P benchmarks. We take a look at part of the latest SPIVA report next.

Table 11.1 is a sampling of mutual fund performance over 1, 3, and 5 years against their respective benchmark. For example, in this sampling of 1,041 large cap mutual funds, 72.72% underperformed the S&P 500 index over the 5-year period ending 2013. That's scary in view of all the attention given to relying on the professional. It's even more thought-provoking when you realize you can now buy the S&P 500 index in the form of an ETF. The story gets worse. Read on.

Table 11.2 shows the percentage of funds from the opportunity set 5 years ago that are still around. So of the large cap funds you had available for investing in at year-end 2008, only 56.87% survived and only 72.72% of those were able to beat their respective benchmark.

In the last couple of paragraphs, I've focused you on performance or the lack thereof. How about style consistency (style creep)? *I spent a whole chapter trying to convince you that style (proxy for size) was huge in terms of portfolio returns.*

Table 11.1. SPIVA, US scorecard 2013[33]

S&P Indices Versus Active Funds (SPIVA®) U.S. Scorecard				Year-End 2013
REPORTS				
Report 1: Percentage of U.S. Equity Funds Outperformed by Benchmarks				
Fund Category	**Comparison Index**	**One Year (%)**	**Three Years (%)**	**Five Years (%)**
All Domestic Equity Funds	S&P Composite 1500	46.05	77.53	60.93
All Large-Cap Funds	S&P 500	55.80	79.95	72.72
All Mid-Cap Funds	S&P MidCap 400	38.97	74.00	77.71
All Small-Cap Funds	S&P SmallCap 600	68.09	87.32	66.77
All Multi-Cap Funds	S&P Composite 1500	52.84	80.38	71.74
Large-Cap Growth Funds	S&P 500 Growth	42.63	79.78	66.67
Large-Cap Core Funds	S&P 500	57.74	80.56	79.39
Large-Cap Value Funds	S&P 500 Value	66.56	76.75	70.26
Mid-Cap Growth Funds	S&P MidCap 400 Growth	36.72	79.37	86.19
Mid-Cap Core Funds	S&P MidCap 400	43.48	67.27	83.94
Mid-Cap Value Funds	S&P MidCap 400 Value	45.33	73.97	67.14
Small-Cap Growth Funds	S&P SmallCap 600 Growth	55.61	86.10	69.60
Small-Cap Core Funds	S&P SmallCap 600	77.70	91.10	74.73
Small-Cap Value Funds	S&PSmallCap 600 Value	78.99	88.00	60.74
Multi-Cap Growth Funds	S&P Composite 1500 Growth	38.14	86.54	68.56
Multi-Cap Core Funds	S&P Composite 1500	62.74	84.51	77.15
Multi-Cap Value Funds	S&P Composite 1500 Value	49.21	70.68	67.98
Real Estate Funds	S&P U.S. Real Estate Investment Trust	50.00	86.71	80.28

Source: S&P Dow Jones Indices, CRSP. For periods ended Dec. 31, 2013. Outperformance is based upon equal weighted fund counts. All index returns used are total returns. Charts are provided for illustrative purposes. Past performance is not a guarantee of future results.

Source: S&P Dow Jones Indices LLC

Table 11.2. SPIVA, US scorecard 2013 (5-year data)[33]

Five Years			
Fund Category	**No. of Funds at Start**	**Survivorship (%)**	**Style Consistency (%)**
All Domestic Funds	3033	74.12	50.51
All Large-Cap Funds	1041	73.97	56.87
All Mid-Cap Funds	516	72.67	43.60
All Small-Cap Funds	662	75.68	55.29
All Multi-Cap Funds	814	73.96	42.87
Large-Cap Growth Funds	339	74.93	59.29
Large-Cap Blend Funds	359	72.42	55.15
Large-Cap Value Funds	343	74.64	56.27
Mid-Cap Growth Funds	239	68.20	49.37
Mid-Cap Blend Funds	137	75.18	45.26
Mid-Cap Value Funds	140	77.86	32.14
Small-Cap Growth Funds	250	73.20	61.20
Small-Cap Blend Funds	277	74.01	55.23
Small-Cap Value Funds	135	83.70	44.44
Multi-Cap Growth Funds	229	71.62	38.86
Multi-Cap Core Funds	407	75.43	51.84
Multi-Cap Value Funds	178	73.60	27.53
Real Estate Funds	142	89.44	89.44

Source: S&P Dow Jones Indices, CRSP. For periods ended Dec. 31, 2013. Charts are provided for illustrative purposes. Past performance is not a guarantee of future results.

Source: S&P Dow Jones Indices LLC

Further inspection of table 11.2 reveals that except for the real estate funds and small cap growth (61.2%), less than 60% of any category of funds maintained their original style after 5 years.

Can you imagine the frustration of an investor who builds a portfolio based on solid principles and finds out he has ended up with a different portfolio from the one he started with? That's like finding out at the finish line that the horse he bet on changed jockeys on the back quarter mile.

Could all these be why my client strategies seemed to underperform? I thought, *No, it had to be me.* The mutual funds had staffs of PhDs, and government and corporate connections. They had people in private jets on the airport runways of faraway places. As the fog lifted, I realized that I had fallen into the average annualized return trap. I hadn't done my homework and really understood mutual fund performance and fees. All those years of paying for their private jet fuel and dinners with government officials suddenly slapped me upside the head. I would not still be in the money management business if the ETF industry had not come along.

I urge you to explore the many differences between actively managed mutual funds and exchanged traded funds. There are good-quality arguments for using either. Perhaps this will be your first test of analyzing data, drawing conclusions, and standing independent of the herd.

Let's end this chapter with a quote from John Bogle, founder and former CEO of Vanguard Group of Mutual Funds.

THE MUTUAL FUND INDUSTRY...

A TRIUMPH OF SALESMANSHIP!

A FAILURE OF STEWARDSHIP!

CHAPTER TWELVE

Pulling It All Together

What Did I Say?

The preceding chapters have been about the history, the numbers, and the tools needed to understand the past and to successfully navigate future stock markets.

In the 1960s, the stock market was about picking good-quality companies that were participating in the growth of the post–World War II domestic and world economies. The United States had a monopoly as a world economic power. Although we didn't know it then, communism was an economic failure. The 1970s and 1980s taught us, the investors, that government could enhance control of the US economy with monetary policy. Market success was then determined by how well you understood and anticipated Fed action. Massive quantities of new investors entered the stock market as tax-deferred savings plans were sanctioned by the government for the first time. From the 1980s till now, we left the post–World War economy and entered the globalization phase of the US economy. The United States no longer has a monopoly.

What I found through my experiences is that the markets, over the decades, may have looked different but were pretty much the same structurally. To be successful in any of them, you needed to understand the emotions and sentiment of the investment public. You needed objective measurements of investor attitude, such as margin debt levels. However, anecdotal evidence of speculation and apathy oftentimes served us well. The cycle of opportunist was alive and well in every market cycle.

The stock market was and is about the flow of money. You will never know exactly how much sideline money is out there. But you need to attempt to answer the questions like "Is there more available money out than in the market?" "Is the current level of money participation nearer a top or bottom in the market?" Understanding the size and location of outside money provides context and is another key measure of sentiment.

Currently, the developed world is worried about debt—primarily government debt. Government debts are today measured in trillion dollars. Although that level is mind-boggling, realize that government income is also in trillion dollars. Don't get bogged down in debt. The stock market game going forward will be about central bank policy and debt, to be sure. But it will mostly be about the flow of international sideline monies. You will need to know how much is out there and which governments are freeing it up or locking it away via monetary and fiscal policy. It may be in the form of exchange reserves or gold bullion or simply money in the vault.

Today, more than ever, the market is about central bank policies. You must track these policies through data. All economic data come from governments. Many pundits run with this data to spin a story or theme that gets you to take action. Sometimes, the wrong action. You must learn to think objectively and independently. You must learn about the sources and types of data available to you. With the creation of the Internet, it's never been easier or cheaper. Understanding data is crucial. It gives you the most objective view of the stock market context. Understanding the context helps you stay calm, improves decision making, and can also help you sleep at nights.

You are going to need technical analysis tools similar to those described here. We are in the global economy now. That most likely means you will be investing globally. You may not have access to data like that available in the United States. What will you do? You will have to rely on technical analysis. Essentially, technical analysis is a subset of behavioral economics. Technical analysis is extremes analysis, and you know the herd is wrong at the extreme. From the Treasury International Capital data, you now know that there are multinational herds of investors. You must track them and their money.

Indicators like Money Flow Index and the summation index tell you the reality on the ground in real time. That's good, but they don't tell you why. It's important to develop experience and trust in the technical tools as sometimes they are all you have to aid you in a decision process. You may or may not find out why later. Understand that most technical indicators don't work in all markets. Many indicators, like the stochastic or MACD, are great in trendless (sideways) markets but prematurely trigger you out of trending markets. I've offered the McClellan Summation and Money Flow Index since I've confirmed they work in all markets.

Finally, to be successful in the markets, you must minimize bias.

Most investors come to the task with preconceived notions about the present and the future. Pessimism and political bias are the most deadly. Don't let the politicians color your view of the investment landscape. Don't try to divine the future either. Rather, focus your energy on the present. Listen to the data and understand that knowing the present context is all you really have and, at times, quite sufficient.

Stay away from pessimists; they've been wrong forever. To paraphrase Jared Diamond in *Guns, Germs, and Steel: The Fates of Human Societies*, a million years ago, when a man came over the hill and into your valley, you killed him. No questions asked. Today, you sue him for trespassing. There has been progress.

As long as mankind wants a better life for his children, progress will continue. Stay optimistic; strive to be happy.

EPILOGUE

What was I trying to say?

The stock market is about political-economic macroforces and intermarket relationships. Within this context, money is moved about by the perceptions of the players attempting to guess the next economic outcome and trying to take advantage of it. A successful investor's task is to recognize shifts in context, identify relevant relationships, and move investment dollars appropriately in terms of timing and risk. He then waits for other investors to be the first to discover his *history.*

As such, the successful investor and his money usually stand alone outside the assurance and warmth of the herd. Always leaving as the herd arrives, it's a lonely, often brutal endeavor!

> *As Jeremy Grantham said when asked, what investors would learn from this financial crisis: "In the short term, a lot. In the medium term, a little. In the long term, nothing at all".*
>
> *As J.K. Galbraith put it, markets are characterized by "Extreme brevity of financial memory...There can be few fields of human endeavor in which history counts for so little as in the world of finance."*

Notes

1. Beebower, Brinson, and Hood, "The Primary Determinant of Portfolio Return Variations," *The Financial Analyst Journal*, 1986, vol. 42, no. 4, 1986 and vol. 47, no. 3, 1991.

2. "Cumulative Wealth Indices of Basic Series," *Ibbotson SBBI 2014 Classic Yearbook*, pp. 232–250.

3. "Growth and Value Investing, Equity Investment Classification," Presentations and Education 2014, Morningstar Principia.

4. "Risk and Volatility, Summary Statistics 1926–2013," Presentations and Education 2014, Morningstar Principia.

5. S&P 500, S&P 400, S&P 600 fact sheets, dated June 24, 2014, at www.spindices.com.

6. "French-Fama Growth and Value Series," *Ibbotson SBBI 2014 Classic Yearbook*, pp. 119–121.

7. *Ibbotson SBBI 2014 Classic Yearbook*, pp. 41–42.

8. US Dollar Graph ID = TWEXMMTH, FRED database, St. Louis Federal Reserve.

9. US Dollar Broad Graph ID = TWEXBMH, FRED, St. Louis Federal Reserve.

10. Gold Fixing, Graph ID = GOLDAMGBD228NLBM, FRED, St. Louis Federal Reserve.

11. S&P 500 Earnings and Estimates Reports, S&P Dow Jones Indices LLC, Howard Silverblatt, senior analyst, various dates, www.spindices.com.

12. Analyst Ratings Network, http://analystratings.net/stocks/NASDAQ/INTC/.

13. Bureau of Labor Statistics, http://data.bls.gov/cgi-bin/surveymost?ln (consumer prices).

14. Baker, Bloom and Davis, "Measuring Economic Uncertainty," Federal Reserve Bank of St. Louis, 2013.

15. Bureau of Labor Statistics, http://data.bls.gov/cgi-bin/surveymost?cu (unemployment).

16. "10-Year Treasury Constant Maturity Rate and Nominal GDP," FRED, St. Louis Federal Reserve.

17. *Dr. Ed's Blog*, "10-Year Treasury Constant Maturity Rate," Yardeni Research Inc., FRED, St. Louis Federal Reserve.

18. Humphrey-Hawkins report to Congress, July 22, 1997, http://www.federalreserve.gov/boarddocs/hh/1997/july/ReportSection2.htm

19. Jim Trimmer, "Understanding the Fed Model, Capital Structure, and Then Some," March 4, 2012.

20. How Equity Supply Impacts Stock Returns in Past 30 Years, TrimTabs Asset Management, February 20, 2014, www.trimtabs.com.

21. Liyu Zeng, CFA, "Examining Share Repurchasing and the S&P Buyback Indices," S&P Dow Jones Indices LLC, FRED, St. Louis Federal Reserve, Moody's Aaa rates, July 2014, www.spindices.com.

22. "Total Assets Reserve Banks & Excess Reserves of Depository Institutions as of November 25, 2014," FRED, St. Louis Federal Reserve.

23. "Total Assets of Reserve Banks & S&P 500 Price Index as of November 25, 2014," FRED, St. Louis Federal Reserve.

24. Summary Statistics of Annual Returns, *Ibbotson SBBI 2014 Classic Yearbook,* p. 100.

25. iShares by Blackrock, June 30, 2014, http://www.ishares.com.

26. BMI Indices, S&P Dow Jones Indices, http://us.spindices.com/search/?query=bmi/.

27. FRED, Federal Reserve Bank of St. Louis, University of Michigan sentiment survey, http://research.stlouisfed.org/fred2/series/UMCSENT.

28. FRED, St. Louis Federal Reserve Bank, Series ID= MZM

    Series ID = H.4.1. Factors Affecting Reserve Balances.

29. NYSE margin levels: http://www.nyxdata.com/nysedata/asp/factbook/viewer_edition.asp?mode=table&key=3153&category=8

    Original data source: FINRA. FINRA is a registered trademark of the Financial Industry Regulatory Authority Inc. Reprinted with permission of FINRA.

30. Treasury International Capital System, http://www.treasury.gov/resource-center/data-chart-center/tic/Pages/ticsec2.aspx.

31. US treasury, http://www.treasury.gov/resource-center/data-chart-center/interest-rates/Pages/Historic-Yield-Data-Visualization.aspx.

32. FRED, St. Louis Federal Reserve Bank, Series Id=Effective Federal Funds Rate and 3 Month T-Bill: Secondary Market Rate

33. S&P Indices versus Active Funds (SPIVA), US scorecard

    http://us.spindices.com/resource-center/thought-leadership/spiva/.

✓ Books That Made Me Think

1. Chande, Kroll, *The New Technical Trader*, 1994

2. Baumohl, *The Secrets of Economic Indicators*, 2008

3. Peterson, *Inside the Investor's Brain*, 2007

4. Murphy, *Intermarket Technical Analysis*, 1991

5. Morris, *The Complete Guide to Market Breadth Indicators*, 2006

6. Hayes, *The Research Driven Investor*, 2001

7. Vince, *Portfolio Management Formulas*, 1990

8. Zweig, *Winning on Wall Street*, 1986

9. Shefrin, *Beyond Greed and Fear*, 2000

10. Klein and Lederman, *Equity Style Management*, 1995

11. Bernstein, *Style Investing*, 1995

12. Biderman, *TrimTabs Investing*, 2005

13. Fosbach, *Market Logic*, 1987

14. Colby, Myers, *The Encyclopedia of Technical Market Indicators*, 1988

15. Options Institute, *Options: Essential Concepts & Trading Strategies*, 1990

16. Roth, *LEAPS*, 1994

17. Bernstein, *Capital Ideas*, 1992

AN EDUCATED MAN HAS CLUES

TO HIS OWN IGNORANCE.

AN UNEDUCATED MAN

HAS NO CLUE!

Index

Disclaimers

The information contained in this book is general in nature and neither represents nor is intended to be specific advice on any investment recommendation. It does not take into account your personal circumstances, financial needs or objectives. Although the data was obtained from various sources and it is believed to be reliable, it cannot be guaranteed. The contents of this book are not to be relied upon as a substitute for professional financial advice.

Asset allocation does not ensure a profit or protect against loss. There is no guarantee that a diversified portfolio will enhance overall returns or outperform a non-diversified portfolio. Diversification does not protect against market risk.

Investments in foreign securities involve certain risks that differ from those of investing in domestic securities. Adverse political, economic, social or other conditions in a foreign country may make the stocks in that country difficult or impossible to sell. It is more difficult to obtain reliable information about foreign securities. The costs of investing in some foreign markets may be higher than investing in domestic markets. Investments in foreign securities are subject to currency fluctuations.

Mutual funds and exchange-traded funds are sold only by prospectus. Please consider the charges, risks, expenses and investment objective carefully before investing. A prospectus containing this and other information about the investment company can be obtained from your financial professional. Read it carefully before you invest.

Dollar cost averaging does not assure a profit or protect against loss in a declining market. For the strategy to be effective, you must continue to purchase shares in both up and down markets. As such, an investor needs to consider his/her financial ability to continuously invest through periods of low price levels.

ADDENDUM

U.S. LARGE CAPS: This asset class is composed of stocks of companies whose market capitalization are often defined as being at least $10 billion.

U.S. MID CAPS: An asset class composed of stocks of companies whose market capitalization is often defined as being between $2 billion and $10 billion and are considered more volatile than large cap companies.

U.S. SMALL CAPS: An asset class composed of stocks of companies whose market capitalization is often defined as being no more than $1 billion. These companies tend to grow faster than large-cap companies and typically use any profits for expansion rather than pay dividends.

Investments in small and/or mid-sized companies typically exhibit greater risk and higher volatility than larger, more established companies.

LONG-TERM U.S. TREASURY BONDS: An asset class composed of long-term securities issued and backed by the U.S. government having a maturity of greater than 10 years.

U.S. TREASURY BILLS: An asset class of short-term discounted securities backed by the U.S. government, with maturity of less than one year. This is a conservative asset class in that prices expected to remain stable or to fluctuate only slightly.

WILSHIRE 5000 TOTAL MARKET INDEX: The Wilshire 5000 Total Market Index is intended to measure the performance of the entire U.S. stock market. It contains all U.S. headquartered equity securities with readily available price data. The index is a capitalization-weighted index.

DOW JONES INDUSTRIAL AVERAGE (DJIA): The Dow Jones Industrial Average is an index of 30 "blue chip" stocks of U.S. industrial companies.

S&P 500 COMPOSITE STOCK PRICE INDEX: The Standard & Poor's 500 Composite Stock price Index is a capitalization-weighted index of 500 stocks intended to be a representative sample of leading companies in leading industries within the U.S. economy.

For a complete description of all S&P indices referenced in this book, please visit standardandpoors.com. Investors cannot invest directly in an index. Past performance is not indicative of future results.

Edwards Brothers Malloy
Oxnard, CA USA
October 2, 2015